MUD & MARRIAGE

MUD & MARRIAGE

A Housebuilding Adventure

by

MANDY CLARK

ISBN 978-0-9930633-0-5
Noisy Bird Books 2014
www.mudandmarriage.co.uk

Text © Mandy Clark
Cover illustration by Kate Northover
www.katenorthover.co.uk
Chapter illustrations by John Clark
Angel illustration and self-portrait by Mandy Monkcom
www.mandymonkcom.co.uk
Design by Catherine Dodds
design@jardinepress.co.uk

Some names of companies and
people in this book have been changed.

All Kevin McCloud quotes are conjured up
from the imagination of the author and are not direct quotes.

For Margaret and Brian Davey

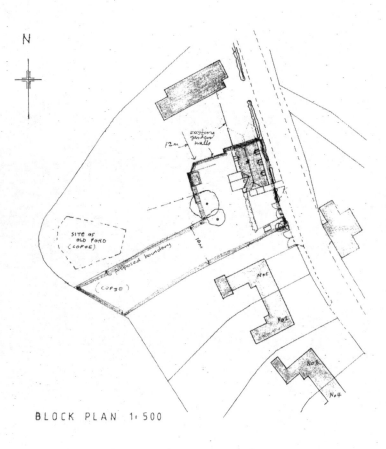

N

SITE OF
OLD POND
(COPSE)

existing
garden
walls

12m

proposed boundary

(COPSE)

No1

No2

No3

No4

BLOCK PLAN 1:500

West Elevation

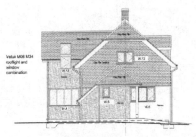

South Elevation

North Elevation

East Elevation

Introduction

If you hold it up to the light you can see the detail in the bird's-eye view photograph of a house nearing completion of its build.

There's a lorry ready to be loaded with the scaffolding that will shortly be coming down and taken away. There are pallets stacked on the earthy site, a rubble pile, the site office shed.

This scene is set in 2008 but the story started back in 2005, when Mr Clark and I embarked on a voyage of discovery to build a life together and to construct our own home.

Along the way I kept a diary and through my scribblings, our memories and my mum's personal journal, the tale of our housebuilding adventure has been told. In all honesty, this is how it was. This is how we navigated the ups and downs of our personal lives which inevitably became entwined with project-managing a house build.

Meeting Margaret and Brian Davey was the catalyst for our enterprise. They helped to set our course, and once we had managed to paddle over the breakers of planning consent, we were out into the open and uncharted waters of building regulations, subcontractors and finance. With its gale-force winds, storms and calm days as well as those glorious but rare plain-sailing days, we were taken to the crest of building hell and back. It was a balancing act between pleasure and pain until we eventually reached the warm shallows; but we survived, despite getting a bit weathered along the way. Mr Clark and I are both wrinklier but wiser, bobbing along nicely on the waves of mortgage payments, waiting to come ashore.

Thank you to all the souls who made it possible for us to live in such a beautiful place, and a note to all prospective housebuilders: just remember the pain fades and one day you won't even think about it. That is until you look through your old diaries.

Part 1

Testing the water

May 2005

15th May

We were idling away on the swing seat this afternoon gazing out over the fields and enjoying the warmth of a beautiful spring day. It's been stupendous, not a cloud in the sky, no crop sprayers, Jehovah's Witnesses or neighbouring DIY to send us rushing indoors.

I've never had a garden of my own before and I'm enjoying it. The red kites whistle away up in the sky and all is well with our world – well, all apart from next-door-but-one's rabbit who escaped and has been sneakily chewing my lupin to bits. It's got me fuming and if he is not stopped I fear he's not long for this world – the pot will be set to boil for this particular Harvey if he doesn't watch out. Actually his nickname is Stewart Granger because I couldn't remember James Stewart's name. Same thing though isn't it? I love that film.

We're living in a small but perfectly formed village en route to the Ridgeway in the midst of the Berkshire Downs. The parish is home to people who have lived around these parts all their lives and, nowadays, to 'fancy London types' as well. We only come from a few miles away but are still thought of as foreigners. The nearest station is around a three-mile drive from here and the trains run regularly to Reading and London so it's very easy to commute. Our home is a rented cream-coloured semi-detached ex-council house with a long garden that backs on to waving fields of wheat.

There are two pubs in the village but sadly no longer a shop. It closed its doors for the last time shortly before we moved here, but there is the Saturday Market in the cobweb-filled village hall most weeks where you can get the paper, your bread and eggs, cakes and plants and suchlike. You can even get a cup of tea and a biscuit for 50p.

Mr Clark's six-year-old daughter – 'the Pickle' as he calls her – asked me today if I was thinking of having a baby. I said that I didn't know. She said that if I was going to have one, could it be a boy. I said I would see what I could do. Then we went indoors and did some tie-dye.

Mr Clark and I are testing the water to see how we get on living together. We've been here for two years now and it seems to be going pretty well. We're even getting married, imagine that. I was proposed to after a splendid dinner at the Royal Oak in Yattendon on Valentine's Day, where, as rumour has it, many years ago a kitchen maid fell through the floor into an old well and was killed.

I discovered that Mr Clark had got the evening all planned. In my Valentine's card he had written a cryptic note that I was to be ready and dressed up by seven that evening. I complained that I had already made an arrangement to meet my friend Amy in the pub after work. I'm a humbug about Valentine's Day but felt extremely guilty as I hadn't even got him a card. So I cancelled Amy who didn't mind too much.

The proposal happened when I had just about managed to rearrange myself after having walked into the door frame of the dining room. It was probably due to the half a bottle of Cabernet Sauvignon, which had slipped down very nicely with my duck, dauphinoise potatoes and baby vegetables. Luckily I didn't hurt myself; embarrassingly I just made rather a loud bang. The maître d' was looking under her eyebrows at me, so I gave the door frame a good scolding and made my way to a white, dumpy and comfy-looking sofa. Mr Clark was wearing a suit and was a bit jumpy so I had a feeling that something was up. I do love a man in a suit, especially if he smells nice. He popped the question and it was all quite emotional really – we both teared up. I thought I'd better say yes as I'm getting a bit long in the tooth and don't want to be too wrinkly in my wedding photos. Mr Clark had the ring made specially. I was very impressed, it really is lovely, and sparkly. And I am very happy because it means he trusts me with his heart.

So now the water is fine, a little choppy at times with a slight north-easterly, but staying on course nonetheless. Mr Clark is, in his spare time, making a garden table out of big old reclaimed bits of wood using his new sash clamps. He's at his happiest when he's making something, swearing away and having a thoroughly nice time.

I'm working at Garlands Organic shop in Pangbourne, which is where I met Mr Clark. He had been coming in regularly to buy his orange juice for a while and I recognised him from somewhere in the dim and distant past. He sometimes came in with his little skippy daughter in her yellow fairy dress. I thought he looked rather handsome and interesting but supposed he must be married. He completely ignored me though, so I didn't speak to him as I thought he was a bit snobbish. One day, however, he came in twice for his orange juice and I had had enough of being ignored, so I approached him by the chiller and said, 'I know you don't I?' He confirmed that I did and later at the till we had a bit of a chat about mutual friends. He gave me his card on which was written 'Mosaic Solutions'. 'Ooh good,' I thought, he makes mosaics, how interesting. Apparently not. He told me he was in IT. I then somehow managed to wheedle his marital or otherwise status out of him. He was single.

Denise and Gabriel, my bosses at Garlands Organic, who had by now become great friends, commissioned me to design and paint their shop sign. I was up on my scaffolding boards making the finishing touches to it and couldn't get the lid off one of my paint pots. Mr Clark was walking into the shop, probably for more orange juice, and I asked him if he would have a go at getting the lid off for me. He couldn't get it off either, so walked off into the shop. I felt a bit bad about it and pretended to be busy when he came out.

I saw him again another day when I was on my lunch hour and we stopped to talk to each other in the street. I told him that I was on my lunch break, hint hint. He didn't get the hint and I thought, 'Well ok, that's it then, he doesn't like me.' Apparently he was just shy. I saw him in the pub after work soon after and he asked me out.

Our first date was on 25th May 2003 at the Swan in Pangbourne. I called him from the A303 Countess Services on the way home from a friend's wedding in Devon to arrange the time.

As a self-employed artist I also need a steady and regular income, so I work part-time at the shop. I feel very sad that Denise and Gabriel will be selling up and moving on soon. That means I will move on soon too. They have been fantastic and always let me take time off whenever I had a big mural painting job to do. I'll really miss them, even Gabriel with his funny ways. He would always be holding forth about something and would go on about the shop being more welcoming if we kept the door open. He made us keep it open even when it was freezing outside, but as soon as he had gone out on his veg box deliveries Denise and I would shut the door.

Murals are going out of fashion and Fuller's Brewery, who I used to do a lot of work for in their pub refits, are using printed graphics now instead. They had to make a few cutbacks and as I was not deemed an essential part of the crew, I had to go. I don't get as many private commissions these days either, so I'll have to think of something else to do.

It's also very sad that we are going to have to move from N° 4 where we've been living. Our landlord told us that he'll be selling the house before too long. I suppose that's the trouble with renting. We feel quite at home here now and the village is such a beautiful place to live, it will be hard to leave.

We stared wistfully up the garden towards the Downs and lamented for a while. What was to become of us? We were only cheered after a bottle of something Australian and affirmed that 'something will turn up'. I feel sure it will.

June 2005

We're getting to know people in the village pretty well. I've been roped into being secretary to the parochial church council. I don't really go to church so it's a bit of a mystery as to how it happened. All I did was go to the pub on 'meet the vicar' night; I had a few halves as he was buying and got nabbed in the back room. I hadn't realised that you must show more resilience to requests from sweet-looking elderly churchwardens as they really are the worst, looking up at you with their little twinkly wrinkly eyes. I'm now on the flower rota for the church too, after having been telephoned. Village life comes with responsibilities apparently. I could stuff my head under the covers and ignore it all but I am too nosey. I'm sure it will be my downfall. Maybe I should stop drinking.

25th June

It's been a beautiful sunny day for the village Flower Festival, I did my quick pencil portraits and raised £25 for the church extension. Not so much but, hey ho, the vicar was happy. After I'd finished his portrait he made me hold it up and shouted, 'Who do you think this is then everybody?' 'Elton John!' shouted everybody. It was true. It was Elton John … in a dog collar.

The festival weekend is being held at the church which is world-famous for its stone effigies of the de la Beche family, sadly defaced in the 1650s by Cromwell and his idiot cronies. Nearly all the effigies have ancient initials carved into them. Lady Isabella has graffiti from 1690 scratched into her and an inscription which mysteriously says 'letters on bodies = old magic'. Laurence Binyon's grave lies in the churchyard too. You know, the chap who wrote that amazingly powerful and emotional remembrance poem *For the Fallen*. Marianne Faithfull's mother, 'The Baroness Erisso', who lived in the village, is also buried in the churchyard not too far from the 1,000-year-old yew tree which is now propped up with a pole.

When the day was drawing to a close and I had put my pencils away, Mr Clark and I were sitting chatting with Margaret Davey, a lovely churchy lady from the village who told us that she has been living here with her husband Brian for thirty years. As we sat there under the gazebo in the churchyard enjoying a nice cup of tea and a piece of fruit cake, she came up with an interesting idea. She had heard that we were going to have to move soon and told us she might be able to sell us a piece of her garden as a possible site for a new house. She told us that she has to raise some funds as her husband, who has Alzheimer's disease, is getting worse and she wants him to be able to stay in the village. He knows his way around and everyone knows him here; if Margaret has to sell their house to pay for his care it would be a disaster. She's invited us round to look at the land.

Margaret said that Brian's Alzheimer's started back in 2000. She had, after some deliberation, eventually gone to see his doctor as he was repeating questions he had already asked and she was getting worried about his memory. He kept losing things too. Apparently he lost the enormous great church key, which was eventually found hanging on a branch of a tree in the churchyard. He lost his baseball hat too, which he likes to wear outside at all times, and Margaret found it hanging from a tree in their garden. Apparently he likes to put things high up, so when he loses something in the house Margaret usually finds it on the top of a cupboard or a bookcase. Apparently he has been attending a memory clinic and also takes part in a research project called OPTIMA (Oxford Project to Investigate Memory and Ageing). In the early days Margaret said that they both enjoyed going to the John Radcliffe Hospital and then getting the bus into Oxford for lunch, but that this was getting more difficult now. Brian is in the care of the Oxford Primary Trust, and Rory, his CPN (Community Psychiatric Nurse), looks in on him every six to eight weeks. Brian hasn't warmed to Rory.

I think Stewart Granger is no more. My lupin has grown back.

Mr Clark's mum and dad have bought us a mower. It must be a relief for both sets of parents to be marrying us off at last.

I think the Pickle has been instructed not to touch me. If I do accidentally touch her she looks very worried. She keeps her arms clamped to her sides. We shake hands, which is allowed apparently.

She came striding up to me on her last Sunday visit and said loudly in my ear, 'My mummy doesn't like you!' Luckily I was kneeling on the floor so I looked her straight in the eye and said (knowing full well that her mum obviously didn't like what I had become in their lives), 'Well … your mummy doesn't really know me properly does she? The most important thing is that we like each other isn't it?' Thankfully she seemed satisfied with my answer. She's so little it makes me feel awful. Mr Clark and I have suggested to the Pickle's mum that we all meet up on neutral ground but she doesn't want to. I can quite understand.

Apparently I am a child-hating man eater. I wouldn't want to meet me either.

I really have been trying hard to be patient and understanding. I even stick up for the Pickle's mum sometimes when Mr Clark is spitting feathers and try to get him to see things from her point of view. Our phone is very resilient; it has been thrown against the wall a few times but still works – well, apart from the numbers 4, 5 and 9 which get stuck.

After all I suppose it is just history repeating itself. My parents split up when I was the Pickle's age and I have a stepmother, so I know how most people in this scenario are feeling. I can see how Mr Clark is feeling and I know that he is a good person and doesn't deserve all the flak. It must be difficult for the Pickle's mum to see him happy with someone else and it looks like she is punishing him for it. Mr Clark tells me that she's the one who wanted them to separate and was in the end adamant that she didn't want him back, but I can see things must be very different for her now that I'm around. She is angry and upset.

My mum took her anger out on the kitchen cupboard doors and that's where I learned the 'f' word.

When my mum and dad divorced, amazingly enough, my mum didn't even know if she could keep us. This was 1970 but apparently in the early 20th century, custody of the children was automatically granted to the father. It seems unbelievable now.

I used to go to my dad's house every Saturday with my brother and sister. He would take us on outings to shops like WH Smith to spend our pocket money and then treat us to a Wimpy for lunch. I remember us sitting on the red padded seats slurping the dregs of our knickerbocker glories with our straws and getting told off for making too much noise. As I remember it, my dad didn't have much patience in those days. I think he was tired and stressed due to commuting to London all week to work in an advertising agency and he could really have done with a rest. Instead he had pests. His dad time was a bit intense and packed into one day a week, so it was no wonder he was a bit grumpy. But he never missed a Saturday and was always appreciative of the clay model offerings I made him. It can't have been easy for Sue either, marrying a man with three squabbling children who'd come and take over her house every Saturday. To be fair though, she did come along on days out and always joined in with our games. Sometimes she made us cry with laughter by putting the stereo headphones on and singing along to folk songs completely out of tune. She always had tea ready just after *Doctor Who* as well.

It's slightly different with the Pickle though. She doesn't have siblings to rely on for comfort and support. I know there is only one of her but she can make enough noise for three. I have a lot of fun with her and her dad playing games, dressing up and suchlike. My mum used to say that she missed us when we were at our dad's as it was so quiet. I expect the same goes for the Pickle's mum too and it is on my mind.

Sadly, my stepmum couldn't have children. I hope that part of history doesn't repeat itself. My self-help books tell me to visualise. So I am visualising.

Thinking about having IVF treatment. I've been researching it on the internet.

27th June

We went round to Margaret's house to look at the piece of garden in question. It's a small plot which consists of little old shed, her vegetable patch and a copse. It certainly looks big enough to build a house on. We will make enquiries to the planners, but it might be tricky as it's in an Area of Outstanding Natural Beauty. We also found out the village is not within a settlement boundary, which apparently might cause a problem.

30th June

Mr Clark's sister Jane, who is a town planner, came along to have a look at the proposed site and has done us some sketches of what she thinks the planners might allow. It seems small, so Mr Clark and I are slightly worried. We are thinking instead that we might take a chance on making the dimensions of the house as big as we need and see what happens.

July 2005

It's a no-go situation with the planners, although they did say that if Margaret sold us her outbuilding, currently used as a garage and store, we may be able to convert it into a house. It's a bit of a tall order but we approached her with the idea and as luck would have it Margaret is brave enough to go with it. At the moment she uses the building to park her car, and store logs and her oil tank, along with some very big spiders. It was built from reclaimed bricks and tiles in the 1970s. There's a greenhouse attached to it with a triffid-like vine growing in it, and a gravel walled garden with raised fruit beds where she grows her raspberries and redcurrants. The swallows nest in her garage every spring so we would have to make sure they aren't nesting if we get to build the house.

Mr Clark's relative once or twice removed is a lovely beardy architect called Bryan (with a 'y') from Wivenhoe in Essex, who, for a reasonable relative's fee, will do us some initial drawings. It's very exciting. I can't help feeling that the odds are stacked against us somewhat but, as my granny used to say. 'A faint heart never won a coconut.' 'Give me the balls,' I say. I suspect that's what she would have said too.

Mr Clark and Margaret are an A1 top team. They have already been to the planning office and are doing all the preliminary footwork and research to find out about what we need to do to apply for planning permission. They are hatching a plan of attack.

Wedding plans are going well. I'm still going to the gym twice a week, and my sister Kate and her husband Dave are coming over from New Zealand to do the catering. We've been making all the arrangements over Skype for free which is a bonus. The marquee is ordered, along with the band, the disco and a magician for the kids. And I've got my dress. I went shopping with Amy and found a very stylish and simple one off the shelf at Coast. I'm keeping it at my mum's and trying it on every now and then. The planning is a military-style campaign. Hairstyles have been trialled – curly-up do's, tousled half-up and half-down do's – but none have done it for me. What a lot of fuss. To fake tan or not to fake tan? That is the question. Support knickers or no support knickers? If I was a proper girl I would know the answers.

I suspect most brides have top table stress. Who is supposed to sit at the top table? And where? I asked Sue my stepmum if she wanted to sit at the top table or with her parents at their table. Actually she was quite chuffed to be invited to sit at the top table, but even after thirty-five years I'm still worried about my mum and stepmum being in the same room together, let alone at the same table. It's also a real task deciding who to invite and who will give us a hard time if we don't invite them. I wonder what will happen when the Pickle gets married.

I've got to have an op. Pah! IVF treatment is very expensive and might work better if I have the op. I won't go into details but it is a something-oscopy. I really hate anaesthetics. They scare me witless – what if I die and never wake up? Why can't I get pregnant? Other people do at my age. I told Mr Clark he is not to have hot baths. He said, 'Bollocks to that.' Am I thinking about it too much? Should I eat more alfalfa?

August 2005

5th August. Lovely sunny day.

I got up at five o'clock in the morning to pick up the wedding flowers from the flower market in London with Julia, the local farmer's wife, who knows all about these things and expertly helped me choose the right ones. We did our own arrangements in the church; me, Mum, my friend Jilly and Julia made a beautiful professional one for the font and another two for the top table.

We all helped to decorate the marquee, then went to The Olde Boar Inn and tried not to drink too much. We saw our neighbour Phyllis there. She told us about the dead man's seat. This is the seat nearest the bar and is usually inhabited by the oldest customer, so when the seat is vacated the next one takes their turn. Phyllis was sitting there smoking away. She has her own little silver ashtray with a lid that she carries around with her. She is very fond of Mr Clark. The chap who used to live at Nº 4 before us is called Steve and she calls him 'Stevie Wonder' in her lovely Berkshire accent. She says she can't decide which of them she likes the most.

We haven't yet joined the BBC (Barred from the Boar Club) but I'm sure we will do something they don't approve of soon. It's only a matter of time. They've barred quite a few villagers over the years.

6th August. Lovely sunny day with white fluffy clouds but a slightly chilly wind.

Wey hey, we got married! Me with no knickers or fake tan and Mr Clark with trousers which were much too long and all wrinkly at the ankles.

Our big day was really great. The Pickle was a bridesmaid and had chosen her own dress and shoes. My best girl, Jilly, who had come over from France with her daughter Laura, was all set to help the Pickle get ready when she got to the house. But as soon as she arrived she went up to her room, shut the door and wouldn't let anyone in to help her. She let me brush her hair though and looked very pretty, much like a little blonde flower fairy clutching her posy of pale pink roses. All the bridesmaids wore different styles of dress in subtle shades of pink and white because I didn't want them matching. Two of the bridesmaids with particularly determined characters didn't get on well, which was a pity as they had to be separated for the photos.

Preparations were going smoothly until I discovered the security tag from the shop was still attached to my dress. We only had about twenty minutes until I had to be at the church, so my sister and I were going to carefully cut it out of the lining with a pair of scissors. Jilly, however, had other ideas and came bounding up the stairs with a rolling pin saying, 'It's ok, we'll smash it off.' I hitched up my dress to find the tag, Jilly hit it as hard as she could with the rolling pin and … SPLAT, out came a stream of red dye. OH. MY. GOD.

Time stood still. Tumbleweed blew across the landing. Jilly and I looked at each other and then screamed. Luckily it had narrowly missed the actual dress but had soaked through the lining and onto the carpet. We had to cut a lot of the lining out and all got very hot and bothered. I had some Rescue Remedy. Thankfully my dad stayed calm, as he didn't really know what was going on and steered clear of the chaos. It was good job I'd been on the champagne already. Jilly went off with my sister and the other bridesmaids and I shakily got into the back of the beautiful blue Cadillac with my dad. We were driven by Jilly's brother, the daaarling Giles, who luckily was as cool as a cucumber. I was very relieved to have got to the church and that a smiling but nervous Mr Clark was waiting for me, that my dress was ok and that people wouldn't worry that I was bleeding to death as I walked down the aisle. Our friend Richard played the organ, the Reverend 'Elton John' Hogarth made some really corny jokes, our friend Deborah read 'I Wanna be Yours' by John Cooper Clarke, and we all sang *Jerusalem*. My shoe got caught in the ragged and ripped lining of my skirt as I tried to get up from kneeling and I heard my sister snort with laughter at the suggestion that all my worldly goods were now also Mr Clark's. The poor man has married an artist but he is very welcome to my pencils and putty rubber should he want them.

At our Superman-themed wedding reception, Boge, the best man, was going to make everyone believe that he had lost his speech for a laugh, and guess what? He really did lose his speech and had to make it all up. Silly bugger.

My dad told a funeral joke. Had this turned into a comedy wedding?

15th August

We have had an exhausting trip to Devon and Cornwall for our honeymoon. Fortunately no one died of the sickness that descended on quite a few of the guests after the wedding. We spent a good couple of days checking up on everyone. Mr Clark's doctor friend Louise explained to us that there is often sickness after a wedding, usually due to the dreaded Norovirus. Mr Clark's dad was poorly but evidently that was due to consumption of booze rather than the wedding bug.

September 2005

Mr Clark has made an extensive survey of roof styles in the village: hips, half hips, gable ends and the like. He has taken photos and put it all on a spreadsheet, and could even be planning to put it all in an article for *Homebuilding & Renovating* magazine. I jest, though actually he did get a letter published in H&R magazine and now we have a year's free subscription. Very useful. He is very thorough is Mr Clark.

We received the plans, which are marvellous. It's a country-style cottage with dormer windows; something like Margaret's house but smaller with around 150 square metres of floor space. We would have liked to go, as Kevin McCloud might say on *Grand Designs*, 'ultramodern with clean lines, stretching the parameters of convention', but it's not allowed round here, more's the pity. How I would love a glass atrium and Mr Clark would be very keen on an orangery.

Downstairs will be mostly open plan. The kitchen, dining room and sun room are basically one big room and the latter has been designed to be mostly glass. Upstairs we will have a big gable-end window in the main bedroom to look out over the fields to the sunset. The frames (screen) for these will be made of oak. There is talk of a steel structure for the house but it may be possible to go for a timber frame, which we would prefer. The upstairs has cleverly been made slightly bigger than the ground floor so we'll have an overhang (a bit like Mr Clark, heh heh) and a cantilevered floor with oak posts as supports.

There are a few changes we would like to make, so we went to Wivenhoe to see Bryan with a 'y'.

We're still living at N° 4 for the moment and as yet have no knowledge when the house will be sold. We haven't been given a date so we'll just hang on in here until we get the heave-ho.

Me, the Pickle and Mr Clark play mermaids on a Sunday morning when she stays over. Well, we are mermaids and Mr Clark is the grumpy pirate who is looking for his treasure which we have hidden. Actually he is the grumpy wet chap in a towel who has just got out of the shower and reluctantly looks under pillows and suchlike with the mermaids shouting 'hotter!' and 'colder!'

We've got a rat in our kitchen. We put some flour down to see where it went and it went absolutely everywhere, swishing its horrible tail. It's a job to know where it's getting in. Mr Clark is on a mission to kill the bugger. He has every known rat-killing device and a fierce determination. He is communicating on a rat forum where people post pictures of their deceased pests. I have to disinfect the whole kitchen every day. We've got those stupid little ceramic tiles on our work surfaces so there's a lot of scrubbing to do.

Mr Clark is wondering about a ground source heat pump.

To do:

- Make a few copies of the plans
- Ring Centre for Alternative Technology re: heat pumps
- Ring Energy Saving Trust re: heat pumps

Things to think about:

- Power points
- Lighting
- Immersion heater?

December 2005

Had the op. On the way to the hospital they were playing 'Don't Fear the Reaper' on the radio. I nearly made Mr Clark turn around and go home. It's all so undignified. The anaesthetist had to come in and calm me down. He said that no one had ever died in his care. I was only slightly relieved but nearly bottled it as I was lying there waiting to be put to sleep. Still, it's over now. Onwards and upwards. Must make an appointment at the clinic.

The Pickle came over on Boxing Day. She and her dad worked hard on a nativity play for which I was the appreciative audience. The Pickle was wearing her blue fairy dress with a cushion stuffed up the front as the Virgin Mary, and Mr Clark as Joseph, the donkey and all the wise men wore a tasteful paisley waistcoat and a tie round his head. I was told off for asking questions, as the audience traditionally would not have spoken. Then the vicar came round for a visit. I honestly can't remember when the house had been in such a mess and his face was a picture as he surveyed the scene, but after all it was Christmas, what did he expect? He picked his way through the debris and found a space on the sofa. He said he was just checking up on his flock. He didn't stay long, probably in case he became entangled in the nativity, literally.

January 2006

Mr Clark has caught his rat and is very pleased. I didn't want to see its horrible squashed whiskery little body. I'm glad it's gone though. At least now we have the most hygienic kitchen in the whole of Berkshire. He posted his picture proudly on the rat forum.

February 2006

We went to the IVF day in Oxford and have had an assessment appointment. Now we know all about it. We were shown a short film and listened to a talk given by one of the top docs in a room full of other hopefuls. Apparently the odds of conceiving aren't good for someone of my age, as was made apparent on the sliding scale diagram shown on the doctor's PowerPoint. Mr Clark and I were then shown into a small room where the finer details were gone through. They say that I'll get bloated. Sounds rough to me. Do I really want to put myself through it all?

March 2006

The IVF drugs arrived by courier last week. I have to keep them in the fridge and I have to squirt stuff up my nose which will apparently turn my hormones off.

To my dismay it is giving me hot flushes and making me feel really ill. I would actually like to have my hormones replaced with something far nicer (maybe a G&T or even a Pimms). I'm working at George Palmer Primary School with their Year 6s on a massive mural project at the moment. The title is 'The Place Where You Live', and it will depict scenes from the local area. We're working hard producing pictures for the miles of corridor walls within their spanking new two-storey building. I'm trying to act normal.

Our landlord has arranged for people to view the house as he says now is the time to sell it. Not good timing really as surely I am supposed to feel like I'm nesting aren't I? I have to grow follicles and suchlike. We could just throw in our plans to build a house and buy this one with its knuckle-scraping Artex-walled kitchen and strange DIY 'posh porch' with freezing cold toilet and noisy light fan thing. We think not. Where will we go? Will we be homeless?

April 2006

My God I feel like shit. How are you supposed to inject yourself with a syringe full of bubble-filled hormone injection nastiness? Surely it's dangerous. My skin is awful. I've got bags under my eyes. They fear I am not growing my follicles properly. It's all really uncomfortable. Mr Clark is being brilliant and dealing with my wobbles in a grown-up fashion. Some women apparently breeze through it with no problem. I am trying to relax by having Jacuzzi baths. Well I say Jacuzzi; the one in this house sounds like an underwater road drill. The bathroom loo has a macerator, which sounds the same.

I can't really believe we paid a planning consultant, who called himself an expert (well he had a suit on), £105 to come to our proposed site to weigh up the chances of us getting planning permission. He said we had an 80:20 chance not in our favour. Well thanks a lot.

We sent in the plans for the scrutinous eye of the planners. £140 just to submit them. Our parish council has recommended the application to West Berkshire Council.

The George Palmer Primary School murals are finished and I have organised an exhibition of the children's artwork in the school hall. The Madejski Stadium can be seen from the school and has been depicted in the mural, so we invited Sir John Madejski to come along to the opening. He said that he would be delighted to attend.

When he arrived at the school in his Rolls Royce we were all lined up to greet him: me, the headteacher and some of the staff and pupils. The headteacher then scooted swiftly off to her office saying, 'You'll be ok to show him round won't you?' I hadn't been primed for this so was a bit surprised.

We all made our way to the hall and to his credit he looked around the exhibition making very encouraging comments, and allowed a picture to be taken for the *Reading Evening Post*. He then went round to each and every classroom where he was mobbed by children all wanting his autograph. I can still picture him signing his name with a pink plastic pen topped with purple fluffy feathers. He must have signed hundreds. He was also bombarded with questions, one of which was from a boy in the classroom from where we had a good view of the stadium. 'You live over there in a flat at the top don't you Mr Madejski?'

'Yes I do,' said Sir John.

'Do you shop at Morrisons?'

(Can you picture Sir John Madejski with his shopping trolley, making his way to the ready-meals section, and at the till chucking in some 3-for-2 tubes of Pringles and a Mars Bar, then making his way back up to his penthouse with a Morrisons carrier bag?)

I think he is a very good chap and the pupils who met him that day will remember his visit for ever.

May 2006

After weeks of chewing our nails over our planning application and keeping our fingers crossed for a favourable outcome, it was turned down. Apparently though, it is possible to appeal the planners' decision by asking your local council's planning committee to decide instead. To do this you need to get your local councillor to bring your case before them, so we will give him a ring and see if he is willing to help.

Brian got lost in Cambridge when he and Margaret had gone there for the day and were planning to go to Evensong at King's College. Unfortunately both Margaret and Brian needed the loo, so off they went into the public convenience and when Margaret came out Brian was gone. The police found him at 10 o'clock that evening (Margaret says probably having a wee against a wall). She had booked into a hotel just in case they had trouble finding him. The police brought him back and apparently Brian was under the impression that they had arranged the hotel room and thought that was a very decent thing to do.

It was the 'Rottweiler incident' that really knocked him for six and into the next stage of his Alzheimer's. He had taken Tanzy, their little Jack Russell, for a walk up at Fayleys Border where she was savagely attacked by a particularly nasty Rottweiler. Brian bravely managed to save her, but she had to be stitched together again. She seems to have recovered well. Mr Clark bought her a squeaky tennis ball to help her get better. Brian hasn't recovered well though. His car has been sold as he would surely get lost if he went out in it now. His bicycle has gone too. Margaret told me that Brian had passed something called the MAVIS driving assessment in 2003 but she had serious doubts about his driving even then and was always trying to hide his car keys. He was given a drug called Aricept around this time which Margaret said helped him quite a lot.

Chris Webber, our local councillor, came over to talk about taking our application to the planning committee. He was very positive about it all and encouraged us to go for it, put the plans in as we want them and ask villagers if they would send in some letters of support.

We went round to see a few villagers with the architect's drawings and talked through what we were planning to do. Everyone we talked to was very encouraging and promised to lend their support. It has been fantastic to get such a response. Mr Clark and I are really heartened by it all.

I managed to grow three eggs. They extracted them and Mr Clark managed to do the business. We waited to see if they would get it on. We hoped they were playing them some Barry White overnight in their little warm and darkened box. I had a lot of pain and at least some hope. We rang the next day and they said two had made it. We were overjoyed. The prospective buyers of the house were mystified at the joy and tears they witnessed as we danced around the kitchen, being careful of course not to scrape ourselves on the Artexed walls.

We went back to the clinic so they could syringe in the embryos. At the clinic they have walls full of baby pictures to show all their successes. The people there were all very lovely and wished us good luck. Really I felt like I should stay lying down and didn't want them falling out again, what with gravity and all that. So I reclined the car seat on the way home and tried not to sneeze.

The wait was awful. I played them Mozart and told them about all the good things that lay ahead for them in their lives. I told them what fun we'd have and that school wouldn't be that bad. How we would be living in a beautiful new house that we'd built …

The test was negative.

We've got a date for the planning meeting at the council.

Chris Webber said that it would be a good idea to give the committee as much information as we can before the meeting.

June 2006

We've moved down the road into an empty musty cottage which is in the grounds of a big house in the village owned by a Mr Allison. He has kindly let us stay for a while until we get sorted out. The Pickle says it smells 'old and dearie'. The building is badly in need of some TLC and is very chilly indoors even in this hottest of summers, but we're really glad to be here. Luckily the Pickle is taking it all in her stride.

Most of our stuff has been stored at Mr Clark's mum and dad's and in my mum's outhouse. The rest has had to be put in one of those big expensive storage facilities.

Mr Clark's mum makes a mean roast dinner which we are invited to share on a Sunday. The Pickle comes too and by dessert she has more often than not slid under the table. She normally sits next to me and kicks me gently. I have a feeling that she is always testing me. The first time I met her I knew that she was a canny chick. I had been invited round for tea at the flat Mr Clark was renting at the time. I remember feeling really nervous as I walked up the stairs and knocked on the door. They made me a cup of tea and she sized me up in the way that little girls are good at, asking me what I liked and didn't like. I had no idea if I had passed the test or not.

There really should be another word for stepmother. It just has 'wicked' in front of it, however hard you try not to think it. We have awkward moments when people assume I am the Pickle's mum. We just look at each other and roll our eyes now.

It is really difficult for me to watch Mr Clark struggling to get to see his little girl, trying to do the best he can with the constant threat of his access being denied. Even though he has to tread his way through the minefield very carefully he manages to have a fantastic relationship with her. I think it is quite hard on the Pickle as she spends so little time with her dad and they have to pack it all into just a few hours. It's just very sad. I can't see Mr Clark dressing up as Batman, however. Corduroy is more his thing.

Margaret has decided to tell everyone in the village about Brian's Alzheimer's, as his behaviour can be really odd now and he walks round and round the lanes and byways, looking down at the ground from under the peak of his baseball hat. Amanda, a friend in the village, rang Margaret one day. She was worried because she had seen Brian walking on the busy B4009 along the white lines in the middle of the road. The people at the pub have told their customers about Brian too so that they can look out for him and not be alarmed by his behaviour. They were also asked if they would bring him home if they saw him anywhere unusual.

Now that his disease is getting so much worse he doesn't have the patience to stop and let Tanzy sniff, as dogs are wont to do. He walks so fast now. The walking seems to be what keeps him going and Tanzy now refuses to go out with him.

Margaret has to go out to regular church meetings of an evening and when she does I sit with Brian in their house. When Margaret goes, he tells me that he will be off to bed and makes his way up the stairs. Minutes later he will come downstairs and into the sitting room where he will tell me again that he is off to bed, so off up the stairs he goes again. This can go on for an hour or so before he actually does go to bed. I give him a drink and some biscuits in between journeys.

I am getting really good at communicating with Brian now and join in with his strange and often amusing conversations. I think the trick is just to go with it, agree with him and not challenge anything he says. He gets very confused otherwise.

Margaret says that he used to be quite a shy man but he really likes to have a joke now. She said that his three pet subjects were football, work and money. I wish I had known him before – or maybe I don't actually. Perhaps it is better that I don't have any memories of him before his Alzheimer's set in. He used to be an engineer and worked on the Jubilee Line for the London tube network. He and Margaret lived and travelled all over the world with his work, and it is said that when he was young he could have been a professional footballer (he had trials for Darlington) but a leg injury had put paid to that.

According to Margaret, Brian has always had his ritualistic habits and would never go out without his coat done up. It's still the same now. He gets very frustrated with the zip of his coat or fleece but lets me help him with it sometimes, although Margaret is the only one who can really get him to do anything. She has to negotiate with him to get dressed properly. He puts his jumper on before his shirt and at night puts his pyjamas over his jumper. She tries to lay his clothes out in the right order but says it doesn't work that well unless she is there with him negotiating all the time. It must be very frustrating for both of them. When he gets ready to go out he takes his slippers off and puts his shoes on and does the laces up. A moment later he has undone his laces and put his slippers back on. Margaret then has to negotiate again to get him to put his shoes back on.

Margaret has received a letter from the memory clinic which says that Brian's score in his last set of tests is low and that his memory is now markedly declining. He doesn't even remember that he doesn't like tea. I make him a cup and he enjoys it. It has to have a lot of sugar in it though. He has an incredibly sweet tooth. That's probably why he doesn't have many left.

Preparations for the planning meeting at West Berks Council are under way. We are writing to all the councillors in the hope that we can nudge them into supporting our idea. Mr Clark does write an exceedingly good letter.

Margaret gives us a good supply of cuttings from the *Telegraph* which keep us up to date about planning matters.

We are having trouble getting our deposit back from our rented house landlord. He is actually an old friend of mine so it's making me feel really awkward. Before we moved out we cleaned the carpets and scrubbed out the cupboards but he still wasn't happy as he had found a couple of cobwebs. In fact the house was much cleaner than when we had moved in. He said that it didn't matter too much about the red stain at the top of the stairs from the wedding dress incident as he could claim on his insurance but said that they wouldn't replace the underlay. He looked under the carpet to view the underlay and discovered there was no underlay. He was bewildered because when the carpets were put down when he bought the house, he had paid for underlay. He looked at us as if we had stolen it, which was the last straw for Mr Clark who then wrote him a stiff letter. We still didn't manage to get all our deposit back. This has made our friendship very tricky now.

Top tip* Never rent a house from a friend.

15th June

Planning meeting – 6 pm.

We sat in the front row; Tim (our parish council chairman), Margaret, Mr Clark and me. We all had our speeches prepared, only five minutes allowed each.

In filed the councillors and the planning police. We sat through two unsuccessful planning applications, the last of which involved a loud bunch of protestors jumping up and down in the seats behind us. It was all very exciting. My hands were sweating.

At last it was our turn and Tim was the first to speak. He told the panel that the parish council were behind the project and had recommended our application. We had nine letters of support and no objections which is apparently very rare.

When Tim had finished, Margaret got up to speak. She started off very well but when it came to explaining the reason why she wanted to sell her land, she faltered and burst into tears. It was very dramatic and some might think it was staged, but poor Margaret sat back down and Mr Clark took over and finished her speech. She wanted the committee to know that her husband would need continued care and support and that she needed to release some equity from her property to maintain his quality of life. She provided a quote from the 'Affordable Rural Housing Strategy' which stated that 'More affordable homes should be built in rural areas, even in National Parks'. She had also written that she could not see how the proposed development would be harmful or intrusive to the environment.

Brave Mr Clark then read out our well-rehearsed plea.

He said that he appreciated the points made by the planning officer and the work that had been undertaken in dealing with our application.

He pointed out that as there is no defined settlement boundary around the village, it is therefore difficult to build new homes. To be able to build would inject new life into the village rather than to leave it to stagnate.

He also quoted from the 'Affordable Rural Housing Strategy' which said that, 'Planning policies stopped the evolution of rural communities and that social issues should be taken into account.' He suggested that more affordable housing was required in rural areas in order to attract younger people into villages.

He told the committee that the development would be sympathetic to the surrounding area and would not be a prominent feature. The location is not in the open countryside and not on a 'green field' site.

He noted that similar applications had been approved in other areas and therefore our development would not be exceptional.

Finally, Chris Webber, our local councillor, took the helm. He made a breathtakingly splendid case for us and his words really hit the mark.

He told the committee that he found himself in an unusual position as normally he would be urging them to reduce development in rural areas. He said, 'I feel that this village is different as it has no settlement boundary and needs to move on, survive and keep its spirit and therefore occasionally development must take place.' He also said that 'the development would help to keep two families in the village' and that he was 'encouraged we had the support of the community behind us'.

He urged the committee to see beyond the planning policies and make an exception in this case.

The planning officer did not like this and argued that personal considerations were not relevant planning considerations. He agreed that each application should be considered on its own merits but only planning merits.

The members of the committee, having been for a visit to the site, agreed that the proposed dwelling would not have an excessive impact on the street scene and was of a sympathetic design. They also said that planning policies should be changed in order to allow more affordable housing in the countryside, and that it should not be necessary for residents to attend a planning committee in some distress in order for an application to be determined.

The members queried whether this application could be treated as an 'exception-site' as generally in rural areas houses could only be built on exception-sites with conditions attached. The planning officer said that this was not relevant in this case as exception-sites were only allowed for affordable housing controlled by social landlords such as housing associations, and there are significant controls on who could occupy the dwellings. Apparently, policy ENV20 was key in this case and he said (through gritted teeth) that if members felt that our application met the required criteria then it would be appropriate to approve the application if they so wished.

It was like the end of a courtroom drama. The councillors looked like they were more and more in favour as questions were bandied about. Luckily, in the end the members felt that our application did meet the criteria in respect of ENV20, but it was suggested that a condition removing our 'permitted development rights' should be imposed if that helped. They said that they felt that the application could be approved.

One by one they raised their hands, apart from one who abstained.

The chairlady announced that our application had been approved and the planning police had faces like smacked arses. I wanted to leap up and dance around the room hooting. As there was no hooting allowed I sat on my hands and bit my tongue. Taking away our permitted development rights is a small price to pay, we can build our house – that's the main thing. We thanked Chris Webber for all his help. What a fella.

We have three years to commence development.

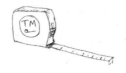

July 2006

1st July. Heatwave.

According to our planning permission we have to retain one and a bit walls of the existing building. There is also a restrictive covenant attached to Margaret's land, which means she has to ask Yattendon Estates for their permission to change its use. Margaret says that this will be just a formality and that she will write them a letter.

Apparently there are such things as 'developer contributions' when building a house, which are imposed by West Berkshire Council; a bedroom tax in other words, and a rip-off and a disgrace according to Mr Clark. This is a sum of money they charge according to how many bedrooms you include in your build. Its purpose is supposedly to offset the fact that you will be utilising local services, such as libraries, schools, open spaces etc. There's a lot of open space around here; I don't see why we have to pay for it though.

Bryan with a 'y' has handed the plans over to another Essex architect called David, who will draw them up in technical detail, and his mate Ken, a structural engineer, will do the sums and specifications for the build.

What luck – we've found a really great place to live while we're building. Boge, Mr Clark's mate, Motorhead fan and best man at our wedding, was painting and decorating at a beautiful, part-17th century, part-Victorian farmhouse in nearby Bradfield, when the lady who lives there asked him if he knew of anyone in need of accommodation. She has a small converted one-storey barn in her yard which is for rent.

We went to look at it and met Barbara, who opened the door. She took one look at me and said mysteriously, 'I know who you are.' 'Oo-er,' I thought. Had she seen me miming backing vocals on *Top of the Pops* in 1990, or had I done something dastardly in the past that I should be feeling guilty about? It transpired that she knows my dad and stepmother really well. She's even got a photo of them on her kitchen wall and a cartoon drawn by my dad in a frame in her hallway. She and her husband used to go sailing with them but sadly her husband has since died. She offered to rent the barn out to us for a reasonable rate in exchange for help such as mowing her vast lawns, watering the vegetable garden, and looking after her horses and dog while she's away.

It's a lovely place. Millions of roses everywhere and lots of grass which just keeps on growing, to Mr Clark's dismay. I will somehow have to overcome my fear of horses.

We moved our stuff in but there isn't much room for my art equipment, so a lot of it will have to stay in my mum's studio. But it is a luxury. Many self-builders have to stay in caravans and mobile homes while they build their houses. I feel very lucky that we can stay here and don't have to live on-site. It'll only take fifteen minutes or so to get to the site from here, depending on how many pheasants, horses, cyclists or tractors get in the way.

We bought a spanking new fridge which immediately broke. It happened just after we moved in, and the weather is really roasting. What a pain in the arse.

5th July. Thunderstorms.

My mum's birthday.

Setting up for the 'Rogues' exhibition at Blake's Lock Museum in Reading. We are hanging our work in the old Turbine House which is now a trendy post-industrial venue and makes a great gallery. It sits over the river Kennet while the water flows along underneath. This will be the third pop-up art gallery with my artist friends Zoe and Lorenzo. It'll be great if I can sell something. Our first two shows 'Winging it' and 'Winging it again' were great but very hard work to get together, what with having to apply for funding and getting the buildings ready. We don't really have a title for this one as it's in a proper venue. It was fun putting on the shows in empty shops but this one feels like we have 'arrived'.

6th July. Hazy sunshine.

The Rogues Gallery Private View. I sold two pictures – a big acrylic flamenco dancer and a small pastel flamenco dancer. Am very pleased. Lorenzo sold the portrait he had done of me with battery-powered flashing boobs. Zoe sold some rude monoprints inspired by a friend who, she had just found out, was a high-class hooker.

$$\oplus \oslash \oslash$$

August 2006

1st August. Cool and blustery.

Off to Dartmouth for few days. I really hope it isn't cold, wet and windy like our normal holiday weather.

While we were away poor Barbara fell over the doorstep of her house and broke her back. I think she will be ok but she is in the Royal Berks Hospital. We went to see her and apparently she is having an awful time as she is getting forgotten about when it comes to pain relief and is in agony. The ward she is on has a really bad reputation. Her daughter has to be there all the time and is trying to get her moved to another ward.

Barbara lets her farmyard out to another farmer for his beef cattle. Poor little things, all standing there steaming and pooing in their pen, just waiting to be big enough to be turned into burgers. Mr Clark is licking his lips but I just look at their lovely big brown eyes, wet noses and long eyelashes and feel very sorry for them.

30th August. Sunny and warm.

I started on another painting of a dancer and have also been commissioned to do some pastel portraits of three siblings.

September 2006

7th September. Lovely day with a fresh breeze.

I have been playing badminton with Mr Clark – well, if you can call it that. He hits the shuttlecock really hard over the net and then I pick it up off the floor. I ping it back over the net, and so it goes on. We're trying to keep fit but I don't know if I can keep this up, I think he'll have to get someone better to play with.

Now that we can build our house, watching *Grand Designs* on the telly holds even more interest and inspiration for us. Mr Clark and I are soaking it all in. It is really useful to have other people's experiences to learn from. They always have trouble with their windows. I hope we don't. Our design isn't so grand though.

November 2006

26th November

Armed with our house plans and a flask of tea, Mr Clark and I went to the Homebuilding & Renovating Show in Shepton Mallet. We had an early start as we wanted to pack as much as we could into the day and catch a seminar on 'The basics of building your own house'. It seems there are three ways of going about it. The first option is to employ a general builder;

the second is to employ subcontractors while project-managing yourself. The third is to do a lot of it yourself and employ subcontractors when you need them. It is a tempting thought that I could take some time out to project-manage the house build. A daunting prospect but it could save us a lot of money.

We had a good scout around and managed to collect a whole library of information in our carrier bag. As we'd really like a ground source heat pump we made some inquiries. The technology is quite simple and seems a great way to make energy to heat your house. You need enough land for the loops of pipe (slinkies) which are buried in the ground. A liquid is pumped around that is warmed up by the earth and this warmth is then transferred to your house. If you don't have enough land then you could have a bore hole drilled, which is extremely expensive. We have been offered differing opinions about whether it will work properly in chalk (which we have a lot of in our area as the village sits on chalk upland). There is a heat pump cupboard designed into our house plans. Earth Energy seem like a good company and Ice Energy have a grid system that you bury instead of having slinkies. Mr Clark didn't warm to Ice Energy as they tried to do a hard sell on us, and he didn't believe that the grid system would work well, if at all.

We ended the day at a seminar given by the building gurus David Snell and Mark Brinkley. They imparted a load of useful information. I took notes but we also bought the *Housebuilder's Bible* by Mark Brinkley and a chart to schedule the build. Exhausting.

I've been working at George Palmer Primary School again, making papier mâché Picasso owl sculptures with the kids during their art week. The results are colourful and fun in spite of the tantrums and the 'I can't do it, could you do it for me Miss?' We got them finished and painted up and I'm really very impressed with their work. We will have an exhibition. I've been working at the school as their artist-in-residence for a couple of years now and I'm very fond of the kids I teach. They are quite a lively bunch, to put it mildly, and we have some good chats. They asked me the other day if I have any children. I said that no, I didn't, and they all looked very sad for me. One girl told me she is going to have three children as soon as she is old enough – she's only nine now. It's a worry. It's really hard as the years roll by and I'm getting older and older. My sell-by date is upon me; if I were a wedge of brie I'd be oozing off the cheese board by now. I've given up on the idea of having children; I have a house to build.

$$\mathbb{D} \ \oslash \ \oslash$$

December 2006

14th December

Apparently it isn't going to be just a formality to change the use of land as far as Yattendon Estates are concerned. They are a big landowner in the area and have restrictive covenants placed on a number of local properties. Mr Clark is furious as it transpires that they want a third of the value of the land now it has planning permission. Why they feel they are entitled to such a lot of money is a mystery. This puts a different slant on things.

Mr Clark took the day off work and we met with Bryan with a 'y', David, the architect who will be taking over from Bryan, and Ken the structural engineer.

It looks like the steel structure originally designed for the house may not be necessary. They have devised a concrete raft construction (reinforced concrete foundations) which means we could go with a timber frame. Lots of measurements and levels were taken before heading off to the pub for lunch. They seem like good chaps, very helpful and efficient. We are a little concerned that they are all the way up in Essex and that it might be difficult to get them here to oversee the build.

Mr Clark wrote a letter to some people in Streatley whose

house had featured in an episode of *Grand Designs*. They have ground source heating and he wanted to find out if it had worked out well for them. They wrote back to say that they were very pleased with the system. He also came across a vast barn (in mid-conversion) in Ewelme on a Pick up Monkeys Ikea delivery. They too had a ground source heating system, so he was able to ask the builders there all about it.

Pick up Monkeys is Mr Clark's current non-profitable business venture. He likes to have an extra business up his sleeve as he refuses to believe that he will be a slave to IT all his life.

Both houses apparently don't have much chalk in the ground around them, so we still don't know if the ground source heating will work for us.

Mr Clark and the Pickle have already made two trial holes to see what really lies beneath our plot. She was pleased to find a treasure trove of several old pieces of pottery and some animal bones. He wasn't so pleased to find so much chalk.

January 2007

I bumped into an old school friend, Nick Hollis, at Drews the Ironmongers. I used to really fancy him with his lovely dark curly hair. I'd always try to sit next to him on the roundabout at the rec at lunchtime. He was a couple of years above me at school but I remember asking him out (what shocking liberation for one so young) and him saying he'd 'sleep on it'. It went on that way for a week, so I gave up. I think it must have been the fags. My friend Louise had made me take up smoking, giving me cigarettes until I eventually succumbed to the pressure. Nick didn't like smoking as it turned out. And here he was in Drews nearly thirty years and seemingly a bit of weather later. I told him about our house build and he offered his building services, so I took his number.

Mr Clark and I have been wondering whether to get a builder to do all of it or go down the subcontractor route. We've given the plans to three builders, V&A Daly, SB Renovations and Ivan Cork, and are awaiting quotes.

NB: According to the *Housebuilder's Bible*, because we are in the south-east our house build cost should be £1,000 per square metre; this varies for different areas of the country.

We have gone through the plans and identified changes to be made. Mr Clark has talked to the architect.

The building regulations drawings have been submitted to West Berks Council and we're awaiting the outcome of their deliberations.

We're waiting for the structural engineer's drawings.

We have now got a geological survey of our land. It is mostly chalk with some clay.

We must get more copies of the plans done and find out more about ground source heat pumps.

Waiting for a quote for drilling a borehole for the ground source heating.

We will use the little and very old existing shed as the site office.

To do:

• Ring the Centre for Alternative Energy
• Ring the Energy Saving Trust
• Get more copies of house plans

We must thank Bryan with a 'y' with a nice bottle of wine.

February 2007

1st February

Paid building regulation fees.

14th February

Romantic Mr Clark made me a superb dinner; duck with a blackcurrant jus, which we ate on a makeshift table made out of my grandparents' old dining room table top balanced on books.

What a chap.

15th February

Sent the solicitor up-to-date plans for the land registry.

We are having trouble finding out about heat pump technology as each supplier has different information. Some people say that it will work ok in chalk, some say not.

We talked to Margaret about the lean-to garage that she is planning to build – now that she doesn't have a garage anymore.

25th February. Lots of rain showers this weekend.

Roast dinner at Mr Clark's mum and dad's.

27th February. Lots of cloud and rain and really chilly.

We went to the Ecobuild Exhibition at Earls Court and had a look at some insulation which was made out of recycled clothes. Very clever and unfortunately very expensive. Mr Clark got given a sample – well, I don't think he was actually given it, I think he just walked off with it. It would be fantastic to build a house that was made out of completely eco-friendly materials; if only they were Clark-friendly prices.

Mr Clark is keen on Earth Energy for the ground source heat pump but is still checking out every single company in the known universe before making a decision.

VAT is something we have to think about now. Is our build classed as a new build? We went to the HMRC stand and talked to someone who wasn't sure but gave us the relevant booklets. Notice 708 July 2002 and Notice 719 May 2002. Looking at the literature we think the house would be classed as a new build and so therefore entitled to 0% VAT.

28th February. Squally showers.

The house has been designed with hanging tiles but Mr Clark and I wondered whether weather boarding would be a better way forward. I suspect we'd have to go back to the planners, so we think not.

Barbara has a friend called H who helps her out with odd jobs. We've been talking to him about our house build and he says he might be able to help us out along the way. He has given the plans to his mate Paul who will contact us regarding project-managing (if we are too chicken).

We had a meeting with V&A Daly round at Margaret's house. Mrs Daly was very bossy and wanted us to have UPVC windows. Ugh. There is no way Mr Clark would even entertain the idea. Mr Daly had a massive hangover so said very little.

The solicitor now has the site plans and has written to Margaret's solicitor to tell them to GET A MOVE ON.

Ideally we would like a rainwater collection system. Boge has set up a company with his mate supplying them. It seems it'll cost around £3,000 for the unit and extra for installation plus probably several pints of beer. We may have to lay pipes by the side of the drains to lead to the rainwater tank or into the rear drain for now.

Mr Clark has started a spreadsheet of likely costs. We're aiming for the build to cost no more than £150,000.

Buildstore, who run the National Self Build and Renovation Centre in Swindon, helped us find a special 'self-build' mortgage and have come up with Skipton Building Society as our lenders. They want to know how much each project stage will cost before they can release any money.

We're STILL waiting for the structural engineer's drawings. We will ring him and kick up a fuss.

When you build a new house you have to pass your Standard Assessment Procedure ratings (or SAP for short). These take into account your energy consumption according to the square metreage of your build, the energy cost rating, the environmental impact and your CO_2 emissions. Well, they could in fact all vary according to how much beer Mr Clark has consumed. Real ale would raise the calculations considerably.

To do:

- Chase up Shore Engineering re: SAP calculations
- Ring TV Energy re: heat pumps and solar panels
- Fill in the forms for water and electricity connections
- Talk to Margaret and get her to chase up her solicitors
- David the architect will chase up the structural engineer

Barbara, now recovered from her broken back, has gone away on holiday and we're holding the fort. Briar, her Border Collie, spends her evenings with us chasing shadows. She spent a couple of hours with her head under the DVD player, tail swishing away, all because she thought she saw one. Mad.

Lambing has started across the courtyard from our house in the barn. Briar likes to give the sheep a bit of a nip. She is fascinated with them but I suppose that's no surprise as it is in her blood. Rounding up is her duty. I can't say I'm fond of lambing – I mean the stuff dangling out and all that. It's ok and a big relief when it is all over and the lambs are born alive, but I feel really sorry for the ones with the wrong colour tabs in their ears, the ones who will be fattened up and sent off. I'm not a vegetarian. That was in fact one of the questions Mr Clark asked me on our very first date. I think if I had been a vegetarian I wouldn't be writing about all this now. Where would I be I wonder?

Briar is a beautiful dog and I love stroking her velvety ears. I wish Mr Clark's ears were more like Briar's; they are quite furry but not all over.

I'm doing my duty feeding the horses and I'm getting quite brave now. I just run in there and run out again, Mr Clark spends his evenings with his spreadsheet and a nice juicy lamb burger.

Mr Clark has been teaching the Pickle to ride her pink bike that she got for Christmas and she is getting pretty good now. They practise in the yard and up the drive at the farm. I think she'll have her stabilisers off soon.

Sometimes we all take Briar for a walk around the countryside in Bradfield and we stop and play Pooh Sticks at a bridge that seems to have been built just for that purpose; the water from the Pang rushes underneath at quite a good speed. We dash excitedly from one side of the bridge to the other looking for our sticks. Mine always seems to get stuck somewhere along the way and sometimes never emerges at all, much to the mirth of my companions. Briar doesn't have a stick. She just likes rushing backwards and forwards.

The Pickle and Mr Clark love to play Frustration together. They get quite competitive, but sometimes they have more of a gentle time and watch a film, and I leave them alone for some quality time together and go and see my mum.

March 2007

7th March. Sunny, warm and spring-like.

Poor Mr Clark has a contract working for Lloyds TSB. Unlike their TV ads the stark chaotic reality is not fluffy round the edges and put to lovely cosy music. He has an ordeal every day and is looking very weary. He doesn't actually have his own desk and has to work at a big table in a room with a lot of other people all shouting away on the phone. He does like his work colleagues, however, which is a real bonus.

We've got the structural engineer's drawings, hurrah. We can't read his writing but hope that it'll all make sense to a builder. He says to ring him with any queries and he'll be happy to help.

NB: All fixings into the oak frame (screen) have to be stainless steel.

We've had a couple of meetings with H's mate Paul to see about the possibility of him project-managing our build. He showed us around a massive manor house that he's renovating. He was not at all sure whether we would be able to build the house within our budget so he had a quantity surveyor friend of his do a costing. £275,000 he reckons (aaaargh! Surely not!).

We have had some quotes back. V&A Daly say it'll cost £218,447 and SB Renovations came up with £220,000. No reply from Ivan Cork as yet.

Oh well, that decides it then. We'll have to project-manage it ourselves.

Margaret's oil tank has been moved.

Nick Hollis came along to have a look at the site. We sat on the breeze blocks where Margaret's oil tank used to be and had a chat about the build. I've given him the structural engineer's drawings for the groundworks and block-work quote. He will do his sums and get back to us.

Our mortgage will be released in stages, and we will only pay the interest on each stage as we use it. It is really important for us to work out the budget for these stages carefully, and as we know nothing, our builder friend Andy Sears has been helping us find out about build costs. *The Housebuilder's Bible* is a great help too.

Mr Clark has cleverly managed to reduce the amount for our mortgage payments by juggling things around on his spreadsheet and adjusting the cash flow.

We may be able to get our first payment from the Skipton by next week. Then the solicitors might be ready and … blimey, it gets all serious and proper.

I could then get on with project-managing the build. I haven't got any work on at the moment, so I'll go for it. In the long run it should save us a load of money.

The stage payments will be for:

1. Foundations
2. First-fix carpentry-timber frame shell
3. Making the house wind-and water-tight

4. First-fix electrics and plumbing and external render
5. Second-fix electrics, plumbing and carpentry, completing the property

The SAP calculations should be with us next week.

15th March. Weather getting colder.

28th March. Grey, cold and drizzly.

We went to the National Homebuilding & Renovating Show at the NEC. I was feeling a bit rubbish with a cold so I didn't do much walking around. Mr Clark did all the scouting about and reported back every now and again to check that I was still upright. We talked to a couple who were on their third house build. They had worked their way up and were now living mortgage-free in a big barn conversion. It really inspired us as they were so positive about self-building. They had sandwiches and a flask of tea, which was very sensible and showed that they were seasoned show-goers. Us newbies had to fight our way up an enormous queue in the expensive and jam-packed NEC café. We had a snoop inside some of the mobile homes that people buy for living on-site. Some of them are very luxurious but very expensive.

Mr Clark managed to get a good haul of pens and even a Lafarge Plasterboard T-shirt, so he was pleased. We stayed in Warwick at the Hilton, using a friend's stored-up Hilton points. Mr Clark, it is rumoured, is descended from Warwick the Kingmaker, so we looked around our fiefdom and had some dinner in a cosy little restaurant. I had a big glass of wine which made me feel much better.

April 2007

Easter Sunday 8th April. A beautiful day.

Unfortunately Mr Clark and I are mowing Barbara's lawns.

Margaret is a lay preacher and she told us that while she was taking the Easter service at the church Brian had walked out during the prayers. People followed him out but couldn't get him to come back in. You just have to let him do what he wants to do now.

Donna, Margaret's niece, and her husband Nigel are coming along next Friday and, with their help, we'll be getting on with operation 'not the swallows' nest'. We'll staple up some shrouding in all the apertures in the building. Sorry swallows and thank you Donna and Nigel.

9th April

We gave the plans to a roofer called Darren who used to be one of Mr Clark's mum's pupils when she was teacher. She said that he was a 'lovely lad'.

I'm aiming to get three quotes for each trade.

Top tip* Get like-for-like quotes if you can.

I asked a company called Quanti-Quote whether they could do us guides to quantities and prices for our build. It seems their software couldn't cope with our build as it is too complex. They also don't do prices, just quantities. We have got a rough guide of the materials needed from Buildstore, however.

Thames Water need us to fill in a stupid form so that we can get connected. They have really crap music while you're queuing on the phone. It's really frustrating trying to get to speak to someone and by the time they answer I have completely forgotten who I'm on the phone to because by then I've put the washing on, done the housework and built a scale model of the QE2.

I spoke to a nice young lady at Southern Electric who said an engineer would ring us back within five days. They have better music.

I spoke to a quantity surveyor in Tilehurst who said he will give us a quote for his work if we get him some plans. He is really busy and won't be able to start on it for a few weeks. He charges £30 per hour. I hope he's a quick worker.

11ᵗʰ April

We passed our SAP ratings with flying colours. If we change the design in any way we may need them recalculated, however.

Ivan Cork came back with a quote of about £180,000 without the ground source heating but including flooring and sanitary-ware.

12ᵗʰ April

Our friend Andy Stone had got us a quote from a builder he knows in Chalgrove. His price of around £154,000 looked very reasonable but we needed to know what it included, so we met up with him on-site and took him to the pub in the village for a drink. Unfortunately, even though he was very helpful and professional, his price didn't include certain items, which when factored in made it a much less attractive proposition.

As we looked at the plans that evening it became apparent that we were meant to have beams in the ceiling downstairs, which was a shock to us – nobody had said anything about beams before. Sure enough, there they were on the drawings, but they aren't in the budget. Bryan with a 'y' was very disappointed to hear we didn't want them. This will mean amendments to plans and structural engineer's drawings.

We're still not 100% sure of managing the whole thing ourselves but we will see.

Still no call from Southern Electric (five days indeed). We will need our temporary supply fairly soon. We've sent off their form.

To do:

- Ring the solicitor to check on progress (the mortgage offer will run out shortly)

It's a mini heatwave. I'm working away getting prices for everything. The spreadsheet is bulging at the seams as is my brain. A bit of refining may need to be done to smooth our perspiring brows.

23rd April. Mild and cloudy.

We are thinking Polish. (As in the people not as in furniture.)

Buildstore say that the build has to be done within two years but it may be possible to get an extension for another year. Three years to build? One would hope not.

We now have a job number for the electrical connection and Andy our quoting officer will come to the site for a visit.

We now have a reference number for Thames Water connection too.

Barbara's gardener Maria will ask her husband, who is a carpenter, if he is interested in our build.

I went to see Julian at McCurdy and Co in Stanford Dingley. They usually work on historic buildings such as the reconstruction of the Globe Theatre (don't y'know), but he said they might be able make the oak screen for our gable end. He said it would be best to make it out of drier oak or the shrinkage would be a problem for softwood window frames. He did me a great drawing of how the screen could be constructed and said to make it in small sections because if it was one long length made out of one tree, it might twist too much. I fear their quote will be beyond our budget though which is a shame.

28th April. Quite warm.

We are in Dorset. It's lovely to be away.

30th April. Cloudy and cooler.

There was an earthquake in Folkestone which damaged five houses.

To find:

- Carpenters
- Plasterers
- Glazier

Nick has given us a price of £22,500 for the groundworks and drainage. We are wondering if it would be best to buy the materials ourselves or for him to supply them. I will also ask him if he has built in a contingency budget for any problems that might arise. He reckons on starting in July which would be fine. I will start my schedule of works on my wipeable wall calendar and try to find out if we have any items with long delivery times so that we don't get caught unawares.

The Building Regs approval is taking its time. We must chase them up.

A tall, roundish and very smart rep came along from Tudor Roof Tiles. They look fantastic but are mighty pricey. He's given me some addresses so that I can check them out.

Earth Energy want a copy of the site plan to work out how many trenches we would have to dig for the ground source heating slinkies.

A nice friendly chap from Southern Electric came to the site. He said that we'll have to have a shroud (a yellow plastic sleeve) on the overhead electric cable to stop anyone dying a horrible death on the roof during the build. He said that if we give them enough notice we won't have to pay, otherwise it will be £250.

A temporary electrical supply will be put at the bottom of the telegraph pole in our garden and at a later date we can put a cable underground up to the house for our permanent supply. He thinks it'll cost £350 for the connection and advised us not to use one of their electricians as they would be too expensive.

I asked Southern Electric about tariffs and deals. We were thinking about Economy 7 as a ground source heat pump uses quite a bit of electricity, but Economy 10 would be best for us because it comes on and goes off at specific times during the day so we could time our heating, washing machine and dishwasher needs for the cheaper time. For now we will be charged a business rate for our electricity.

We're having trouble finding a carpenter. A friend recommended a chap called Kieran and says he is reliable. Another option is to have the timber frame made off-site and brought along and then plopped into our existing walls. We have found a great company called Solo Timber Frame who are extremely helpful and good communicators (a rarity I have found so far). They can also make roof trusses which can be pieced together on-site, but that could be pretty expensive.

I rang Kieran who is ill in bed. His wife said he will ring us back when he is better.

I'm getting quotes for:

- The sewage-treatment system (we may need 'consent to discharge' from the Environment Agency)
- Window frames (in both soft and hardwood). Aspect Woodworking say they can also do the staircase
- Roof trusses (made off-site)
- The oak screen (made from dryish oak). Oakwrights are very expensive but I'm sure it would be fantastic
- Scaffolding
- Skips

To do:

- Talk to NHBC and Zurich Insurance
- Look into prices for insulation. Kingspan do foil-backed insulation boards. Compare like-for-like U values (heat-loss values) with other brands, maybe Celotex
- Think about securing the site and moving the shed

We have had several differing opinions about fitting window frames into the oak screen. This is tricky because of potential movement of the oak. Some are scaremongers who suck air through their teeth and shake their heads. Others have ingenious solutions. It's all very confusing.

May 2007

Meeting with Nick: Groundworks.

He will:

1. Clear the access, take out some of the laurel hedge and put down scalpings (bits of waste quarry stone, not Red Indian trophies) to make a hard standing for lorries to drive onto. Also allowing for clearing any debris away

2. Deconstruct the roof and interior walls, dig up the floor and construct the concrete raft. He has allowed for the cement to be pumped in by a cement pump lorry to make life easier

3. Brick up Margaret's garage and make the brick plinth for the timber frame to sit on

4. Do the drainage

5. Install a Klargester Biodisc sewage-treatment tank

6. Get the steel made that connects the chimneys

7. Build the chimneys

We will work out stage payments for him.

19th May. Aprilish sort of weather, a strong cool wind and warm sunny spells.

My friend Debbie gave me a jade face roller for my birthday. I hope it works.

The poor little Pickle is having anxiety attacks and demands to be taken home quite often now on her dad visits. She gets anxious and then feels sick. We've been trying to work out why it has come on so suddenly, as she seems to have been quite happy until now. Her dad tries to talk to her about it but she doesn't really know how to describe how she feels and as he doesn't get to spend a lot of time with her, it is very difficult to find out what to do to help her. I remember when I was young I used to get a feeling of being anxious and homesick even when I was at home, so I do understand. I think it must have something to do with your parents separating and, as a small person, having to deal with the fallout.

We have made the Pickle's room all pink and pretty and tried to make it a relaxing and fun place to be. Perhaps she is anxious about being away from her mum. I had that to deal with as well but I only ever stayed for two nights at my dad's house and that was when my mum was in hospital. It wasn't good. There were monsters under my bed and I had to leap from the door to the bed so their horrible hands wouldn't grab my ankles. I'm sure my dad and Sue tried their best with us and I remember getting up and going into the sitting room as I couldn't sleep. They were watching something funny that I obviously wouldn't have been able to understand as I was only six at the time, but I laughed when they laughed in the hope that I wouldn't be sent back to bed. They must have seen right through my ruse but let me stay up anyway. The Pickle has always stayed overnight on her visits, but won't stay over any more. Naturally Mr Clark is upset.

I remember going on a camping holiday to Swanage with Dad and Sue. I was five and having a really hard time being away from home and just to prove it I pooed myself in the sleeping bag, and not a solid poo either if you get my drift. Poor Sue had to clean it all up. Oh the shame. (I still get reminded about it now). I was eventually cheered up with a Penguin biscuit and a game of Pontoon with my siblings. I was lucky I had my brother and sister there with me. The Pickle doesn't have the back-up that I had in that respect and I suppose that's why she doesn't come on holiday with us either. I go and stay with my dad and Sue all the time these days as they live in Devon and I am purportedly a grown-up. I still have my memories though, good and bad, but that's the way of things isn't it? I still don't like going camping though.

We're looking into getting site insurance and the warranty. Self-Build Zone look good as they do both. They can also do the building inspection and sign off the build at each stage, so we won't have to have anything to do with West Berks Council. This policy could be combined with a warranty inspection, very handy but should you put all your eggs in one basket? (We may get show discount from hearing about them at the Homebuilding & Renovating Show.)

I bought a meter box from Jewson and was astounded at the price – £65 just for a plastic box. Mr Smith, an electrician from the village, will come and fix it to the telegraph pole and put in the sockets; Southern Electric will then come and connect them up at a cost of £405.38.

Top tip* Mr Smith said to me that during the build I must always check the work somebody has done before they go, and get them to explain to me what they have done.

We received a quote from Thames Water for £1,152.00 for our mains water connection. We sent off the form and payment making sure they understood there was no contamination of the site as it is just a domestic garage that we are dealing with rather than a commercial garage.

Mr Clark and I met with Kieran on-site and he will do us a quote for all the first-fix carpentry. For the second fix we will have to specify types of doors etc. so we will have a think about it and do some research. Perhaps we could do some of the second-fix carpentry ourselves.

FYI: First-fix carpentry is the timber frame skeleton of the house including stud walls, roof truss and floor joists. Second fix comprises of things like door linings, doors, skirting, architrave and cupboards.

Am talking to plumbers (when they bother to ring me back).

There is no mains drainage in the village so we will need a sewage-treatment tank. Mr Clark has done a lot of research and has decided on a Klargester Biodisc system. There are six versions of the BA model. The prices range from £2,620 to £3,140. He thinks we will have to go for a version with a pump although you can also just rely on gravity to expel the treated water. Nick will have to measure up and work out the invert level (this is the ratio of distance to fall from the house to the Klargester tank).

It's fantastic really – little micro-organisms eat your poo while they merrily go round on discs which look like big records. When they have done with it (I don't know actually what they do with it), it turns into sludge which sinks to the bottom of the tank. The water that subsequently flows out of the discharge pipe is apparently clean enough to drink (only in desperate circumstances I would imagine). Then that makes its way to a soakaway. The Environment Agency say that it must drain one metre minimum from the water table and to do a percolation test as outlined in the PPG4 information sheet. Apparently the

Geological Society should have information about the depth of the water table in our area. It is unlikely that we will need consent to discharge but it could take up to four months if they decide we do need it.

We have chosen the loos, sinks, the bath and the shower and will be getting them all from Bathroom Whorehouse – whoops I mean Warehouse. The white stuff was quite cheap apart from the bath, which is a sturdy enamelled steel bath. No squeaky plastic baths for us thank you.

David the architect will make sure all the windows are standard sizes so that we don't have to get them made specially. Jeld-Wen windows seem to be pretty good. They supply casement windows which are what we want.

The structural engineer and the architect say they will be available if we have any queries during the build. The drawings we have aren't working drawings, so if the subcontractors need more detailed information we can apply to them for more detailed drawings.

What about the steel feet for the exterior oak posts we are having? Can you get them ready made? Ask the structural engineer and also thank him for all his work.

In order that work can start on the site we need to:

• Get the services connected
• Mark out the site
• Secure the site (should we hire fencing or buy it?)

Kieran says he will get us a quote for the timber frame by the end of the week. We're trying to get a complete document together so we know exactly what he is including and not including. He is proving to be a bit slippery on that front. We'd like him to sign a document but he seems reluctant.

Apparently the mortgage is all cocked up. I despair.

The solicitor called. He has exchanged contracts but there is a problem as the mortgage is in Mr Clark's name only and the deeds are in both our names. Apparently this won't work. They will have to both be in Mr Clark's name for now. Why he didn't notice it when he looked at our mortgage offer is a mystery. It will take the Skipton two weeks to rearrange it all.

I had to sign a waiver for the time being. Am a bit miffed.

I need to get it in writing that the Skipton will accept the Self-Build Zone Warranty. The Skipton say it is for Buildstore to accept Self-Build Zone and Buildstore say it is for the Skipton to accept Self-Build Zone. They should sort themselves out.

I've got my Jeld-Wen window catalogues which will make exciting reading.

Kieran the carpenter's quote is apparently in the post. He said it will take him eight weeks to build the timber frame. I said that we would like him to start mid-August.

The Skipton say that they will accept any warranty as long as it lasts ten years.

To do:

- Get quotes for insulation
- Ring Darren the roofer
- Ring Kieran the carpenter
- Get quotes for underfloor heating
- Get plastering quotes
- Get samples of bricks
- Ring another electrician or two
- Ring another plumber or two
- Find out prices of skips

23rd May

The temporary electrical supply was connected. The chap who came along to do it told me that it was his last day of work before his retirement, so I gave him a couple of chocolate Hobnobs to celebrate and he looked very happy about it all as he slurped down his mug of tea.

25th May. Very sunny and warm.

H said he is happy to help project-manage when needed for £25 per hour, but we're not sure the budget can handle it. He said he will get all the stuff we need for the water connection to the stand pipe and put it together for us.

He will need to get:

- A tap
- Copper pipe
- MDPE pipe (blue medium density polyethylene water pipe)
- Connectors

June 2007

3rd June

Mr Clark's birthday.

My mum's friend Clive has lent us some orange plastic fencing for the building site so that Brian doesn't fall down any holes.

To do:

- Order a digger from Newbury Tool Hire for H to dig the trench from the house to the road for the temporary water supply, and to make test trenches around the site to see what the substructure consists of

5th June. Sunny and warm but a chilly breeze.

PERCOLATION TEST 1 (apparently it's the best of three)

What you do is:

Get your darling husband to dig two small trenches and then mark 150mm on a stick. Next put the stick in one of the trenches and borrow your neighbour's hosepipe and fill it with water up to the mark on your stick. Act like you are a very important scientist on an important mission and wait. Don't be tempted to wander off and miss the moment.

Trench 1: It took 46 extremely boring minutes and 20 seconds for 150mm of water to percolate into the ground. Luckily it was a lovely sunny day. I used the stopwatch on my phone and put my results on my clipboard.

Trench 2: It took 41 minutes and 50 seconds and lots of dashing between trenches for 150mm of water to percolate into the ground. What excitement.

All this is done again for percolation tests 2 and 3 over the next two days and there you have your average.

We are waiting for a breakdown of costs from Kieran the carpenter.

We went to the Build Centre in Swindon and had a good old snoop around. They've got a café which is always a bonus as Mr Clark always likes a cake stop if we go out. We talked to Buildstore who will try to speed up our mortgage amendment. At the Build Centre they have a cutaway model of a concrete raft construction which is very interesting. It's amazing what I find interesting these days.

Kieran will come for a site visit.

I redesigned the oak screen for the upstairs bedroom and the downstairs sunroom windows. It is now simpler than Bryan with a 'y's drawing with more window and less window frame. I found a picture in the *Homebuilding & Renovating* magazine of what I think it should look like. Mr Clark is in agreement.

Kieran recommended a friend of his who can supply and make the oak screen. He will give us a quote and meanwhile I will get on with finding prices for the window frames.

We are now insured.

The plans have been finalised. I got five copies and laminated the original.

Chris Pike from Klargester came to the site. He says that we will need a BA 750 Biodisc with an IPS pump of 50 watts. I wonder if Mr Clark will agree. He said that we need a pipe to take the pumped water out to the rainwater drain at a depth of 400mm. The Klargester unit is 2 metres wide and we will need to dig a hole 6 inches bigger all round. It will need a concrete base and some concrete to fill in around it.

Top tip* Use a watering can full of sand to mark out where your drainage pipes will go.

15th June. Cloudy but warm with a couple of showers.

Work commences, yeaah. H came and dug the trenches. The trench for the water connection has to be 750–1,350mm deep and have one inch of pea shingle in the bottom. Thames Water will charge us £81 to come out again if they deem it unsatisfactory (robbers). They said that they will come out and have a look.

I rang Self-Build Zone. They have sent our documents and my name isn't on them. (I'm starting to get a complex) and it seems we are insured for £16 billion; they apparently need to do something about their system.

Our building inspection will be done by a company called BBS. They will visit after each stage of the build and, if all is well, issue our certificates. They need a set of plans and will then come and do an initial inspection. They told us that we will hear from them in a couple of days and meanwhile will send us a form to fill in. We can't start work until they say so.

Thames Water came for their inspection and luckily Mr Clark was on-site to meet them. I had been detained chasing an escapee sheep down the lane in Bradfield. Luckily Briar the Border Collie was on hand to help and the sheep was saved.

We passed the Thames Water test, phew.

Mr Clark wrote a stiff letter to the solicitors. One of the head honchos said that he would look into the cock-ups that have been made.

We must thank David the architect for all his hard work. It did cost a bit to make the changes and get new drawings, but we think it's good to get all the essential points sorted out now instead of making mistakes further down the line.

To do:

• Make sure the front door is standard size
• Send BBS the new floor joist plan

We are waiting for approval from West Berks Council for the changes and are hoping they won't ask for new structural calculations.

23rd June

Mr Clark and I went to the Homebuilding & Renovating Show at Newbury Showground. I caught a glimpse of Michael Holmes from H&R magazine. He is very tall and handsome, so I tried not to stare. We saw Hayley from Solo Timber Frame and she will do us a quote for:

• The timber frame
• Insulation
• Plasterboard
• Oak screen and windows
• Other windows including the Velux windows

We talked to a company called Nu Heat as we wanted to find out about the possibility of having an air source heat pump. It's an interesting option but apparently they don't work well if the weather gets too cold, so some more research needs to be done. The café at the show was outside and the weather was particularly squally, but we managed to stuff down a bacon sandwich and a cup of tea nonetheless. We talked to Heritage Tiles and Midland Slate and Tile. Ashbury Multis seem the best option for our roof so far. We managed to get a good haul of pens which is of course always a bonus.

We are comparing prices and U values of insulation to go in the studwork timber frame.

- Warmcell (cellulose)
- Thermafleece (sheepswool)
- Isonat (hemp cotton)
- Metisse (recycled cloth)
- Sheffield Insulation (Rockwool)

I'm afraid Rockwool won out due to the insulation value and cost. It is the best value for money, not very eco though, which is really disappointing.

I've got some addresses to look at for the Ashbury Multi tiles given to me by the cheery curly haired chap from Midland Slate and Tile. His name is Mike Chillery, so obviously now we call him Chili Palmer (played by John Travolta in *Get Shorty*). He said that he will send us some samples and was very friendly, efficient and smelled nice.

We now have a schedule for the groundworks from Nick.

1. Demolition/floor slab 2–3 weeks
2. Walls/brickwork/chimney up to first floor
3. Trenches for the ground source slinkies
4. Chimney up to the roof (incorporating the steel support)

To do:

- Tell Nick that we want to keep some of the top soil as it is good stuff
- Ask him about a lock-up for tools
- Give him the measurements for the driveway
- Ask reclamation yards if they would like to buy our tiles

No word from Mr Smith the electrician. I keep leaving him messages.

I spoke to the British Geological Survey and the chap there said that actually the Environment Agency should have information about the depth of the water table. Looking at old records though, he reckoned that it would be between 80 and

100 metres down. I put the information on the Environment Agency's form and sent it off.

We must get the electricity disconnected from the existing building.

I think we will have to get another electrician as we can't get hold of Mr Smith.

I am busily checking out Portaloo hire.

My mum's friend Clive who is a tree expert popped along to advise us about the trees we have on our site, especially the big ash tree. I am concerned about disturbing their roots when we dig the trenches for the slinkies. He said that as a rule you shouldn't dig further in than the canopy of the tree.

We have strimmed the site.

Mr Clark subcontracted Barbara's lawns to a friend of his, but there was an unfortunate incident one afternoon when he accidentally knocked over her stone sundial and it broke. What a pig's ear. Barbara is understandably very upset because I think it holds a lot of sentimental value for her. We feel really bad about it and will get it fixed. So it's back to mowing the lawns again for us. Oh well.

We'll be getting our tile samples from Midland Slate and Tile this week apparently. How exciting.

I spoke to Thames Water who said that they might have to close the road to connect our mains water. I really hope they don't have to as I don't think it would go down too well, especially with our local farmer as we don't know him that well. He looks a bit grumpy and I don't want to tangle with him. Thames Water have to give the council one month's notice for a road closure.

To do:

- Buy a garden gate for the new bit of wall between us and Margaret
- Get felt for shed roof repair
- Get more tile samples

As there is hardly any mobile signal at the site we are looking into getting a temporary phone line put in with BT. In order to do this we need to register our address with the Royal Mail, which means we have to register the house with the local authority first. Then get the plot number from the deeds and a scaled site layout in relation to the public highway. Apparently BT need four weeks' notice. We have to send all the information to their 'New Sites' office in Oxford and then they will send someone out for a site visit. It costs £124.99 for a minimum of 12 months and then it is the same again when we move the connection to the house. What a faff.

29th June 2007. Hot sun, strong wind.

We got the new policy from Self-Build Zone and are no longer insured for 16 billion, which is a shame.

July 2007

1st July. Big fat dark clouds with bits of blue sky.

Bad flooding up north according to the news.

5th July. Cold with lots of rain.

Took my mum to Waterperry Garden Centre for her birthday. What a washout.

I talked to the structural engineer about the steel feet for the oak posts. He said they don't actually have to have shoes as such, they could just have angle brackets to connect to the supporting brick plinths.

The Environment Agency has granted us the permission to discharge from the Klargester. Hurrah.

How long is the lead time for the Jeld-Wen windows and do they come with hardware?

The road won't have to be closed for our water connection. They will have a STOP and GO chappie. I hope the tractors can get past.

We haven't had our tile samples from Chili Palmer. I left him a message to say so.

I rang an electrician I had found advertised in our parish magazine and he invited me round to his beautiful big house in Tidmarsh. 'He must be doing alright,' I thought. We went through a rough plan of lights, sockets and data and aerial connection. Also smoke alarms, shaver points, towel rails, immersion heater supply and outside lights. He seems very friendly and efficient (probably expensive though) and said that he would come along to disconnect our electrics in the building the next day at 5 o'clock. And do you know what? He did. He's got his logo on his shirt and he dresses all in black, just like the Milk Tray Man. And all because...the lady is a tad impatient and wants to get on with it.

NB: All electrical sockets and switches now have to be at regulation heights in accordance with BS 7671 part M of the building regulations for England and Wales.

Unfortunately, after doing our sums, Solo Timber Frame's quote came out too expensive and we were unsure of getting it just right as we have the remaining wall to consider, which likely as not won't be square and straight and needs complicated fixings which they don't do. If we were starting totally from scratch and our roof wasn't so complicated I think we would have gone for it.

And ... OMG I forgot about the oak post by the front door. That could be an extra £100.

Kieran's quote is better – still quite expensive, but as no other carpenter seems to want to quote for the work, what are we to do? We aren't sure the budget can handle it but he said he would go through the prices with us. Mr Clark is scratching his antsy head about it all in a Stan Laurel fashion. We still need a detailed breakdown of what exactly Kieran has included; he did offer to tell us as soon as he can during the build if there are any essential extras.

Mr Clark's friend Toby will come and fit the Velux windows for us, and Adam from Peppard Building Supplies has given us a price for each window. We have asked Toby if he is available for second-fix woodwork and he said he will have a think about it.

I had a bit of a tricky conversation with Darren the roofer. He said quite forcibly that he doesn't think he would like to just tile the roof, he would prefer to batten it too. I didn't know that roofers did that, I thought the carpenter did. How am I supposed to know that, I've never done this before? I don't want to piss him off at this stage though.

NB: The first-fix carpenters put on the vertical battens and then the roofers attach their horizontal tile battens.

7th July. Hot sun with big white fluffy cumulus.

Barbara has had a very small boy pony come to stay and Dotty, who is a girl pony, and a lot bigger, is now totally in love with him. She follows him around everywhere. Poor old Fergie, her regular companion, has been usurped by a very small upstart who isn't actually wild about Dotty's intentions anyway. Briar keeps an eye on them through the fence and follows their every move. She would love to get in there and round them up.

Ron from Heritage Tiles came along to the site with his samples. I now know quite a bit about his family. An hour and half later he buzzed off and I was left with a dilemma and a dazed expression. Mediums or reds? Hmm. I asked my neighbour what he thought. 'Don't know, they both look the same to me. Does it really matter? Get the cheapest.' Good advice Mr Baker.

To do:

- Get Heras fencing to secure the site
- Get prices for scaffolding
- Get prices for Portaloos

We bid £60 for some blue fencing on eBay and we got it, hurrah!

We have got our roof tile samples from Chili Palmer. Very lovely they are too. Now we can show them to Karen Buckingham at West Berks Council for approval and request a site visit. Chili said that he would talk to her if there is a problem. What a nice chap. Lovely hair …

We have to decide on the hanging tiles soon before I go completely mad.

We must tell people in the village about the water connection to warn them of delays.

We went on a jolly to Hambledon to have a look at some Ashbury Multi tiles on their old museum. Very nice too, as was the dinner and a little glass of something in the pub. We bumped into a couple of my old friends there. One of them is an architect who gave us more clues on where to look at interesting tiles in the village.

Our neighbours recommended a plasterer called Sean and he has given us a quote via text message. I have asked him for a written one. He says that really he needs to see the building first. I see what he means but we've got to try to get our spreadsheet in order ASAP.

We will be using a resin injection system to tie the existing brick walls to the timber frame with metal rods. How many fixings do we need, what type of resin do we need and how far do you drill into the wall? There doesn't seem to be a spec for these in the drawings. The structural engineer will send us one.

Mr Clark has seen some great wood-burning stoves which might do for the kitchen. Some of them have small ovens. He is keen on Clearview Stoves as they are well designed and British.

We have decided on A1 loo hire for our on-site toilet needs.

Am working on getting quotes for scaffolding. I must get Kieran to show me on the plans where he needs his lift height.

NB: Lift height = the level to which the scaffolding is built.

We may need an extra lift for the roofer and netting as it is near the road. We don't want anyone falling off into the path of a tractor, or, God forbid, Mrs Farrington in her BMW convertible.

Do we want wood finish Velux windows or white? Another dilemma.

Nick can start the groundworks in the first week in August.

Kieran the carpenter can't start until mid-September.

Our architect David is getting married in October to an American lady in California. He will be away for a while so I hope we don't need him.

16th July. Sunny and warm.

We will need to purchase some Tyvek Housewrap, a breathable waterproof membrane which is used between layers in the walls and the roof.

We bought some second-hand Heras fencing with feet for fencing off the front of the site. We will get a chain and padlock too.

I tried to register the house with the local authority naming and numbering department. There is only one lady in the whole of West Berks Council who can do this and she is on holiday. When I eventually get hold of her she will inform:

- The Royal Mail
- The Valuation Office
- The Land Registry
- The emergency services
- The Council Tax Dept
- Electoral Registration
- Planning
- Environmental Services

So she will be worth her weight in gold as I wouldn't want to be arsed with all that. But is it all worth it at the moment just to get a phone line?

Maybe we could get a signal booster for the mobile phone.

Did you know it costs £50 just to change a house name? I couldn't believe it.

We've got a Buildstore trade card which really seems next to useless as not many people accept it. It's a shame because we are partial to a discount.

Top tip* Use your best negotiating skills to obtain a good discount from your local builders' merchants and other suppliers. You could save a lot of money.

To do:

- Ring Earth Energy, who have given us a quote for the ground source heating. We really do need a guarantee that it will work in chalk

Get prices for:

- Guttering
- Scaffolding
- Rockwool: one pack = 2.4 square metres
- Celotex: one board covers 2.88 square metres
- Tyvek Supro per roll

It is a possibility that we will not have a ground source heat pump as we don't really have enough land. Mr Clark is disappointed.

20th July

Crikey, the heavens opened and they stayed open for quite some time. Clancy Docwra turned up with a grab lorry to fill a hole they had made to connect the water pipes. It was quite a task as the hole was now under at least a foot of water. I was mighty impressed as they did their underwater tarmacing.

It rained and it rained and I was getting slightly concerned now that the water pouring down the road was up to the rim of my wellies. I waved the Clancy Docwra boys off and waded up to my friend's house for some reassurance, only to be met at the door by a frantic Debbie with an empty ice cream tub. She thrust it into my hand and led me to the cellar. Water was pouring in as fast as we were bailing it out. It seemed a never-ending task. Was I going to be here for days? When would the rain stop?

Two months' worth of rain in one day. It finally stopped about 3pm.

After some cheese on toast and some dry borrowed clothes, I braved the ebbing flood. Luckily my car hadn't been swept away. I saw the neighbours who doubted that I would make it home as many roads were flooded. How was Mr Clark going to get home from work? Would we ever see each other again?

A soggy Mr Clark appeared back at home much later that evening.

Kieran says he will know his start date by the end of next week.

Oh yes, I'm now on the mortgage. Good. The solicitors have waived their charges for the changes. Quite right too.

Nick will be starting the groundworks on 6th August.

I've ordered the Portaloo.

According to instructions from the structural engineer and the sketch SK01 provided, the resin fixings will fix the timber frame to the wall and we will need:

- Threaded rods
- A resin gun
- A drill, to drill halfway into the brick (one must blow all the brick dust out of the hole prior to filling it with resin)

We took the greenhouse down and sadly the triffid vine had to go. The weather was so squally that I'd had enough by teatime, so poor Mr Clark was out there in the cold until it was dark. He was blue and shivering when he returned home for his dinner. What sort of summer do you call this?

We have fenced off the boundary. Mr Clark borrowed a whumper from Barbara at the farm and whumped in lots of posts and then tacked Twilweld wire mesh to them. We also moved the shed out of the way, panel by panel. I'm getting a good set of muscles on me now – I'm like Charlie Dimmock. (With a bra that is – I'm not about to let my bosoms swing free. Well, 'swing' is probably a bit of an exaggeration ...) Mr Clark nailed it all back together again and we put some new felt on the roof and made a floor out of paving slabs. It only has a couple of leaks. We congratulated ourselves on doing a job together without arguing too much. It'll be GHQ. I've put a laminated sign over the door saying 'SITE OFFICE'. I'd like to get more signs but Mr Clark is tutting over the bulging budget as it is. Apparently you don't have to have signs but you do have to display your public liability insurance certificate. My laminator is going into overdrive.

Hanging up in the site office I've got hard hats and hi-vis jackets. I've got a first aid kit, an office chair, a paste table, a desk, a fire extinguisher, goggles and an accident book. The laminated plans are pinned to the shed wall. The tea, coffee and biscuit tin are at the ready.

Mr Clark's sister Jane gave me her old steel toecap riding boots as I was complaining to her that Mr Clark didn't care about the safety of my lower digits. He really couldn't see why I wanted to spend money on boots. I was hurt. I can't function without my toes can I? And after all he'd married them too.

Oh the sleepless nights I've had tossing and turning over the choice of roof tiles. So many choices and so many roofs to squint at. I feel a little self-conscious having a good stare at other people's houses. What must they think? Perhaps they think we are private detectives as we do our drive-by photographic shoots, with Mr Clark going as slow as he can, trying not to look suspicious.

We've fenced off the rest of the site to keep Tanzy the Jack Russell out, and also, sadly, Margaret's husband Brian, who is getting steadily worse and who I don't want injured on-site.

We have picked all of Margaret's redcurrants and can now dig up the plants for her and flatten the raised beds. She makes fantastic redcurrant jelly. I hope she has plans to make some more.

The orange fencing scares our neighbour Bridget's horses witless every time they go past, especially if it flaps a bit in the wind. Silly things, they're so easily spooked.

Mr Clark is now keen on getting a wood pellet boiler so we went to Welwyn Garden City to a wood pellet boiler company. The boilers are really interesting in technology terms and are well designed but not really powerful enough for our heating needs. Ideally they would need to be at least 15 or 16kW.

We need to get some reclaimed bricks. I will get Nick to give me an idea of the required quantity and we'll go to a reclamation yard to seek some out.

We are now on normal rate electricity as the 'business' has been taken off it.

I spoke to Adam Jarvis, the building inspector. He needs 48 hours' notice to come and look at the excavation.

The Pickle asked us the other day if you can catch Alzheimer's disease. We assured her that you couldn't and she's much happier now when Brian is around.

31st July. Summer is here.

Karen Buckingham from West Berks Council teetered along in her high heels. I suggested she might want to borrow my wellies but as a seasoned council planner she deftly negotiated the terrain. She ok'd the tiles and the bricks. Karen only works one day per week and if you miss that you're out of luck.

I have been flattening the rest of Margaret's raised beds with a spade and fork. It seems such a shame. Margaret has kept some of her redcurrant bushes and given some away. Everyone keeps telling me not to do the work myself and to let the builders flatten them if they need to. My sister would say I'm bossy and fussy but I would say that I just know my own mind and am a bit particular. I'm on a mission to get the site completely ready you see and they can't stop me. I've put stepping stones made of concrete slabs over the muddy bits.

Brian went for respite care in a home in Shiplake. He escaped a few hours after getting there, but they managed to get him back and rang Margaret the next morning to inform her of Brian's Houdini-style transgression.

Shockingly, Briar the Border Collie nearly died as she had eaten rather a large rubber toy which was obstructing her workings. She had an operation to remove it which saved her at the last moment. We are all really relieved.

Mr Clark and I went to Cirencester to a fascinating reclamation yard to find some oak mantelpieces. We had a really good look around and found loads of oak from an old French barn. Choosing two good pieces was the tricky bit as we were spoilt for choice. Eventually we decided that we would have the piece we'd been sitting on for the kitchen, having stopped for a rest in the sunshine. On our next scout about we discovered a smaller section with an interesting knot in it which we thought would do nicely for the sitting room. The beams will be cleaned up and oiled and they will give us a call when they are ready. On their office wall we saw a letter from Liz Hurley saying how much she loved her reclaimed pieces. If they're good enough for Liz they're good enough for us.

August 2007

4th August

Luckily it was a beautiful sunny day for Mr Clark's mum and dad's golden wedding anniversary garden party. Speeches were made, cake was eaten and everybody was happy.

This is how the build should go:

- Groundworks and brickwork
- Timber frame ground floor
- Scaffold
- Timber frame first floor
- Roof truss
- Chimney up to the top
- Fascias and soffits
- Roof and windows
- Paint fascias and soffits
- First-fix electrics
- First-fix plumbing
- Floor insulation
- Pipework for underfloor heating
- Put in soil pipes
- Screed (a levelled layer of cement which makes the floor)
- Insulation and plasterboard
- Cut out holes for power supplies and light switches
- Plaster inside
- Outside render
- Guttering
- Second-fix carpentry
- Decorating
- Stairs
- Kitchen and bathrooms
- Second-fix electrics
- Second-fix plumbing
- Driveway
- Garden
- Move in

Part 2

Building the dream

6th August 2007

Start of the build and our second wedding anniversary.

I am installed in the site office.

Nick and his mate Ben turned up at 7.45 am and got on with it. They have made great progress and I have found out, in true *Grand Designs* style, that I am pregnant … and I haven't even met Kevin McCloud.

I rang Mr Clark at work to impart the news of the miracle conception. He was so shocked he nearly choked on his Fruit Shrewsbury biscuit. I am joyous but scuppered. Only yesterday I'd been lugging great heavy paving slabs about. I was all set to help with the demolition but now I'm sitting in the shed twiddling my thumbs and staring in a daze out of the window which now looks onto what appears to be a bombsite.

Our neighbour Bridget had ordered a digger for herself today too, so it was very confusing when it turned up this morning as I thought it was ours. The road was chaos for a while as it was completely clogged up with lorries and diggers, but we sorted it out in the end.

Nick got carried away and took out too much hedge for the site access. I'd only popped out to get some milk (boys and their diggers). I should have marked it out instead of just saying, from here … to here. A lesson learned.

Thinking about it, Kevin McCloud should lend himself out, or maybe his procreative vibes actually pass through the telly waves, who knows?

I have spent a merry afternoon knocking nails out of battens. No more lifting for me.

Nick hurt his finger, so I came to the rescue with my first aid kit and then wrote it down in the accident book.

7th August

The Portaloo arrived. It was a nice green one to blend in with the scenery. It arrived on a truck whose registration exclaimed 'LOO4POO'. Mr Clark calls it the Turdis.

We also have a skip. I am not fond of skips since I opened up the side of my car like a baked bean can on one a few years ago. I am steering clear.

Mr TST Scaffolding came along in his brand-new dark red Jag, very spick and span and smelling of some rather classy aftershave. He said that we will have a quote soon.

Ben has taken down the internal walls with a lump hammer. He went a bit askew on some rubble in his digger and toppled over into the back wall making quite a scar on the brickwork. Luckily they had left the ceiling joists in place as support while they worked, but I still thought the whole building was going to come down.

Mr Clark wants to keep the wormy old rafters for some reason. (There is talk of a tree house.) They are being put at the end of the garden.

I must find out what size flues we are having before Nick builds the chimney.

Nick dug up the concrete floor with a pneumatic drill which was very noisy and dusty, so I stayed in my shed with the door shut and the radio on until it was safe to come out. Then the rubble which was put on the driveway was taken away by a grab lorry and now there is a nice pile of bricks ready for Mr Clark to clean up. We have kept the old garage door as he wants to make a wood store out of it, and all the salvageable roof tiles have been stacked up by the garden wall. We can't reuse them in the build but we might be able to get some money for them.

Adam Jarvis from BBS came along in a pristine crisp white shirt and very shiny black shoes, without a coat, even though it was pouring down with rain. He made a very speedy inspection of the footing excavations and steel reinforcement mesh. All is present and correct, so we will get our next stage payment. I would have liked to ask him some questions but he was in too much of a hurry. Not even the offer of a nice cup of tea and a chocolate Hobnob would persuade him to stay.

Nick and Ben are working really hard and we are very impressed with progress. To keep the wall-and-a-bit from falling down they attached some long rafters crossways and have also put boarding all the way round to contain the concrete for the floor slab. Watching the concrete being poured in was very exciting. The concrete mixer lorries had a bit of trouble backing in, which was a bit stressful as the road outside is really narrow and I had to watch out that they didn't take out our neighbour's fence. I also had to try to appease the tutting drivers who were annoyed that we were getting in their way, but it's all done now and lovely and flat.

It is a good job that we didn't have the timber frame made off-site as the slab is an inch wider than on the plans in the toilet/ lobby area. It hasn't made it look any bigger, however, and we are wondering how we are going to live in a house that small.

15th August. Torrential rain showers.

The site is a sea of mud but apparently the concrete is set enough to cope.

I regularly remind Ben that I WANT my pear tree. It has a few less branches since he has been here. My red and white safety tape is no deterrent. The biscuit tin is depleted, and it's not just the builders. We have a mouse in the shed. I must get a mouse-proof container and also a bargain size bag of sugar.

Mr Clark has spoken to a Polish builder called Waldemar who is an acquaintance of our friend Paul the sweary Polish Prince. Some of his gang do tacking (putting the plasterboard up) and plastering. We went to have a look at their work which looked great.

I'm feeling very sick and am finding it hard not to tell anyone about the baby. I think a few people are suspicious as I'm not drinking wine and I'm looking a little pale. It'll be the size of a small shrimp now. I'll be the size of a whale soon. Mum won't be happy. She doesn't understand why I want to have children, although she had three of her own but says that's different. I think she'll be ok about it though.

September 2007

Mr Clark had a robust conversation with Kieran the carpenter. He keeps cancelling meetings and doesn't answer emails or messages. He now says that he can't start until 1st October. It is very frustrating and now my wipeable wall calendar will have to be changed. I'll ring Darren the roofer to let him know of the delay and hope he is ok with it.

Mr Clark is now super-keen on having a wood pellet boiler – he just has to find one that is powerful enough. We will research where to buy the pellets and look at the cost. It seems like a good answer for the heating and is apparently very eco-friendly. It'll do wonders for our carbon footprint.

We ordered the Klargester Biodisc.

13th September. A gorgeous warm sunny day.

There's still no improvement with the Pickle. Mr Clark says that when he goes to pick her up from her mum's, she clings on to the drainpipe and won't let go. No amount of persuasion will get her to go with him. He is very worried and upset.

Brian went for respite care in Farringdon and escaped again. He just followed someone out of the door. He looks so normal, you wouldn't really know that he wasn't just a visitor. He banged on some poor unsuspecting lady's door. The house must have looked a bit like his own, so he thought he was home and demanded to be let in. The lady was so frightened that she called the police. He was recovered, and the care home rang Margaret to say that they couldn't cope with him and could she please come and fetch him?

15th September. Blue sky and warm.

I have got tonsillitis.

Darren the roofer said that he is available in January. If we are ready and have all the materials on-site, he could possibly get started over the Christmas period. Good man.

The damp-proof course (DPC) has been put in and two layers of bricks have been laid, on which the timber frame will sit. Adam Jarvis from BBS will come and have a look before Kieran starts. Apparently we have to put down another damp-proof membrane (DPM) before the screed goes down.

The fireplaces have been made from breeze blocks and our oak mantelpieces have been installed. They've been covered in DPC plastic to save them from the weather. It looks odd having the fireplaces in already, but very exciting as I picture myself sitting with Mr Clark all snug on the sofa looking into the flames of our wood burner.

The drainage has been laid and the Klargester Biodisc has arrived and is enormous. I thought it was the wrong one at first as I was under the impression we were having the one with a smaller lid.

Top tip* Take photos of where your drainage pipes have been laid for future reference.

◍ ⊘ ⊗

October 2007

I had a miscarriage. Apparently the baby had died at nine weeks. Am a bit of a wreck.

Mr Clark has been fantastic and took over the site management while I recovered at my mum's. I had a very dizzy trip to the site to see our newly installed Klargester Biodisc. Mr Clark said that it was a good job I had missed the last episode of the gung-ho Nick and Ben, as I would surely have got a little stressed trying to save my trees and shrubs. It all looks very earthy and flat, but miraculously my pear tree is still standing. The Klargester is in the wrong place which is my fault really, as when Nick had asked me where I wanted it I had said 'about there will do', not realising I wouldn't actually be there to oversee the installation.

Top tip* Mark everything out exactly where you want it in case you aren't on-site when the work is done.

Apparently we had a freak whirlwind at the bottom of the garden while I was in repose. A huge leylandii tree had come crashing down and taken out the garden fence just by next door's cesspit. Clive came along with his chainsaw and chopped up the tree for us. At least we won't go without firewood for a while.

7th October. Cloudy.

Back from a short break in Devon where it had been warm and sunny.

We went to a stove place at Winkleigh airfield and were captivated by a very good-looking Italian wood pellet boiler/ stove called an Olivieri. It puts out 14kW, which will just about do for our underfloor and water heating. Mr Clark had seen one on the Stoves Online website previously and was already enamoured with it.

16th October. Mild, wet and gloomy.

Mr Clark had to help to right a sheep in the field at Barbara's. It was one of her old toothless sheep with a woolly fringe and looks a bit like a muddy Mick Hucknall. She had fallen over and couldn't get up (the sheep, not Barbara), so the farmer from Rushall Farm up the road came to fetch her and took her away in the back of his pick-up truck.

17th October

Kieran and his inscrutable mate Andy started the timber frame. There was some umming and aa-ing and scratching of heads, and some 'Your architect has got this all wrong', but they soon got going. Adjustments will have to be made but I am assured this is par for the course. We have to have the regulation 2ft 9in-width doors for disabled access for the front door, toilet door and kitchen door.

Kieran doesn't drink tea, he has hot water. For lunch he has a tin of fish and a carrot. I don't know if he is slimming or what. Andy has the obligatory coffee with two sugars, doorstep sandwiches, crisps, half a packet of chocolate biscuits and a fag. Andy seems to be in charge and Kieran, in the words of someone I am married to, is the ballet dancer.

It's really exciting to see the walls going up. I am so glad to have this project – it's saving me from dwelling on things. My jeans fit again now and I have flung my gigantic bra in the bin. Kieran has got a house rabbit. Maybe we should get one.

I tidied up in the shed. I can get in the door now at least. I haven't been very shed-proud recently. It is really good to have it all back in order.

I've got prices for softwood window frames to be put into the oak gable end screen and side window. We have, however, met a chap from Wivenhoe in Essex who can make them in oak for the same price. He's a friend of Mr Clark's sister and his name is Chas Crocker. He is very posh, a real craftsman and, as luck would have it, said that he can make the frames in January just before he heads off to Thailand.

The search for a plumber isn't going well.

Darren the roofer came for a site visit with his bouncy daughters who had loads of fun rummaging through my shed and playing with the wind-out tape measure. He said that continuous nib tiles are easier to work with and that we will need bonnets, valley tiles and eaves guards. I don't know what they are but will find out. He needs to know the pitch of the roof and requires the scaffolding to be up to gutter height. I think he must dye his hair. It is very black.

Malcolm from BLR Roofing came to the site for a meeting. He suggested that we look at the Clayhall range of tiles and will get me some samples. Hmm, perhaps Clayhall mediums and reds? I prefer traditional mix and red myself, it just depends on the price. He also might be interested in buying our old tiles.

Malcolm says that Darren is a great roofer but a bit uppity.

19th October. Glorious sunshine.

Brought Mum to see the site and then had tea with Margaret in her garden. I had to spend the afternoon endlessly throwing Tanzy's soggy tennis ball or risk being barked at incessantly.

Measurements on the plans aren't matching up and Kieran and Andy have requested a meeting with the architect, but I think we'll have to manage the build without him coming to the site as it'll cost too much to get him down from Essex. I know it seems a bit mad, but he and the structural engineer are pretty good at getting back to us on the phone if we have a problem.

Due to regulations requiring disabled-access door widths for the downstairs cloakroom, the door will now have to open outwards as there won't be enough height inside the room due to the sloping ceiling.

A1 loo hire will be emptying the Turdis weekly. Margaret lets me use her loo though which is much nicer. She lets me use her landline phone too, which luckily has a good range and works in the site office. I take her messages for her.

24th October. Cloudy with a chilly wind.

Kieran and Andy not on-site.

25th October

Kieran and Andy not on-site.

I gave some plans to Clive's brother, Mr Sparks, who is an electrician, funnily enough. We'll see what price he comes up with.

I also sorted out the good tiles from the broken ones that had been taken off the original roof, and Mr Clark sold them on eBay. The chappie who came along only took the ones he wanted, so now there's more rubble to get rid of.

30th October

Kieran was here this morning and we moved his wood out of the way so that the trucks and lorries don't have to drive over the drain covers to get in. He says that he will finalise the joist plan and hopefully put the order in tomorrow. I asked him to not put his fish tins on my rubble pile.

I went along to see the supplier of the oak screen at his workshop. I had a good look at the posts, which Kieran and Andy will put together on-site. They look great to me and are well seasoned, which is a bonus.

The measurement from slab to ceiling is, at the moment, 2m 53.3 cm, and we have specified 2m 20cm for the finished height including insulation, screed and flooring. This could be a very tight fit, so we will look into getting thinner insulation, with the same U value, for the floor.

November 2007

9th November

It's getting pretty chilly now but the weather seems to be holding out. Lots of sunny days and blue skies.

Kieran put the phone down on Mr Clark. Mr Clark was not impressed.

We have a bit of a delay as Kieran is waiting for Travis Perkins to get the floor joist plan done. He has no idea when this will happen and when he will resume works. It is a mystery as to why he hadn't got it done before now. Another lesson learned. It's a tricky balance between letting your subcontractors get on with it and poking one's nose in. In hindsight I'd definitely poke it firmly in.

The site is at a standstill.

What to do? Communications with Kieran have broken down. He is a tricky one. Some communication would be better than no communication even if it is just to report that he's still on the case. To be in limbo is not what we need at this point.

13th November. Autumn gales, showery and a bit chilly.

Feeling glum.

The strain has got to Mr Clark, what with the Pickle and his stressy job, the miscarriage and now the disappearance of the carpenters.

18th November. Cloudy. The rain set in and then turned into a snow shower.

There was a knock at the door yesterday evening. Strange, we thought, who can this be? We live in the middle of nowhere you see. It was Kieran, who boldly said, 'I've come to face the music.' So we all sat down together, the music was faced and the problems were ironed out. The joists will apparently be with us on Monday. We're having TJI joists which are the thing to have these days so we are told. They are made from engineered wood and are light but very strong. They won't expand or shrink, which means that our upper floor will never creak. Usefully, they also come with pre-drilled holes that you can knock out to put pipes and wires through.

I rang BLR Roofing. They had been broken into so Malcolm was sounding a bit dramatic. I will leave them to it for a bit but I have to decide on the roof tiles soon. 70% traditional mix, 30% reds? I just don't know.

We have chosen Nu Heat to supply everything for our heating system. I wasn't sure about underfloor heating at first as I like radiators because you can stick your bum on them when it is a bit cold or dry your undies if it is raining, but Mr Clark wants it, so we will have it. Nu Heat will work out the zones for the system and the best way to separate them out.

Barbara is away again and we are keeping an eye on her animals. Fergie, the ancient horse with arthritic knees, fell over in the mud and couldn't get up. A lady had spotted him from the road and she came and knocked on our door. Mr Clark and the lady had quite a struggle to get him standing again as it was so slippery, but they managed to get him upright in the end. Poor Fergie, he has to have cod liver oil in his feed to help with his knees but I think it's just old age and that happens to everyone.

We have been instructed to give Barbara's ancient sheep some sheep cake when it looks like they might need more. This is a feed which looks more like a big round millstone than a cake. The sheep give it a lick and apparently they get all the nutrients they need from it. Perhaps we could get one for the carpenters.

⦶ ⊘ ⦸

20th November. Lots of rain but not too cold. Thunder.

21st November

The TJI joists arrived. Kieran and Andy are back on-site and have started putting them together.

Nick and Ben cut out the windows in the existing walls very neatly and rebricked around the edges. They finished the day by making some very wonky plinths for the oak support posts to stand on, as they built them in the half-dark. They might have to be redone.

Clive came and winched the fallen tree stump out of the ground.

Nick and Ben have now also built the chimney up to the first floor. We have been advised by Philip, the flue expert from Stoves Online, to have pumice flues, which are quite expensive but apparently what we need. While they are being installed they will be packed around with Vermiculite insulation.

To do:

• Get door frames for front doors

Mr Clark and I have our regular meetings. Poor Mr Clark – just what he needs when he gets home. I have to time it right, just after dinner and before he falls asleep on the sofa. Sometimes we have our meetings in the pub so we don't have to cook dinner ourselves. We go there with a pact not to talk about the build but it always gets broken.

December 2007

The woodwork is looking good. We're up to the first floor with a couple of walls built already and it's starting to look like a house. We've got three carpenters on-site as we have a Bob now too, who is great and gets on with it. I must say they are all doing a fantastic job.

You can stand on the first floor and look 360 degrees all around you. The views are spectacular. It seems a shame to put the walls and the roof on. It's completely breathtaking.

We have specified Glulam beams to tie the roof together. Kevin would now explain to us, with the aid of an open book resting on its lengthwise edges, what might happen to the roof if we didn't put beams in the right place for its angle; at this point he would let go and the book would collapse flat. Glulam beams (glued laminated timber) are very strong and made from smaller pieces of wood glued together. They can be made for long spans and can take heavy loads; this means our roof will be safe. The beams will also make a good-looking feature in our roof space upstairs.

We've got scaffolding. I didn't see one of their workmen hack down some of my pear tree but I wish I had. I'd have given him an earful. I only looked away for a second or two.

We still haven't found a plumber.

We've got all the Jeld-Wen windows now, unglazed and primed. All we have to do now is paint them. It makes me tired just thinking about it. Barbara says we can use her old stable at the farm as our painting room. It's a bit draughty and ratty but it'll do nicely.

The electrician's quote was actually very reasonable and he looks so smart in his shiny black van.

We have a new building inspector now, called Martin Jackson, who is a cool guy and is very relaxed but knows his stuff. He seems pleased with progress. He came along in his wellies and raincoat and had a cup of tea.

Mr Clark and I have been painting window frames in the freezing stables.

Top tip* Never get your window frames ready primed as ours came with the glazing bars all stuck to the frame. It took us days to prise them off and sand them all down. Either get them unprimed, completely finished, or of course buy expensive windows which are primed properly.

Mr Clark and I have also been painting all the fascia boards and soffits ready for them to be put up. It's been really icy and we've been working inside the shell of our new house, but there are no windows or doors in yet. It's not at all conducive for drying paint and keeping at all happy. I had my boiler suit on over my clothes and my padded Parka over that. I commandeered Mr Clark's hat with earflaps but the cold still gets through. My hands seize up in the mornings; it takes me ages to get my fingers to unfurl. My face doesn't unfurl all that quickly these days either.

I think Kevin would be proud of our 'dedication and resolve' at this point though.

To do:

- Send a joist plan to Phil at Nu Heat
- Order a skip
- Buy a new diary
- Buy more paint brushes
- Paint window frames

The electrician will give us some numbers for plumbers.

We are still waiting for a design from Nu Heat for our underfloor heating system. Once we have it, we can then decide which pellet boiler to go for.

Nick and Ben have built the chimneys up to the top, incorporating a big steel structure that had to be specially made to hold them up. They are really happy because all went according to plan. There was some worry that the angle of the flues wouldn't fit the aperture given for the chimney but all was well. I hope the flue angles will be easy enough for the chimney sweep to clean. We will also have to get cowls to stop those mischievous jackdaws stuffing things down the chimney pots.

There was a problem with the positioning of the chimney as the architect had drawn it in the wrong place on the first floor plan. The ground floor is smaller than the first floor. The first floor has the overhang and is bigger. The architect had drawn the chimney bang in the middle of both floors on the plans, which meant that when it was built, the chimney on the first floor was over to the right somewhat. Yes, really.

Kieran had made the opening for the chimney where it was indicated on the drawing. Nick called Kieran an 'old woman'. Kieran was not happy.

The carpenters have now completed the upstairs timber frame and roof truss. They are building the dormers now. I quite like the open-plan effect of the rooms but it'll be better with walls really.

We should have had a topping-out party but it just passed us by. Oh well.

I've been spending a lot of time at roofing companies. Darren the roofer was the one who recommended BLR Roofing to me, as that is where he gets all his supplies. They were great and would always make me a cup of tea until the day I decided that I would only get the hanging tiles from them, as I had found a supplier that actually had the roof tiles in stock. This would mean far less faffing about and less in haulage costs if I needed more tiles as we went along. Then there was no more tea and it all got a bit frosty. I tried to point out that some business was better than none, but they didn't see it that way and really couldn't be bothered anymore, so I took my business to JJN Roofing who had nice warm offices and were amazingly helpful. I'd like to think I'm a hard-nosed bitch but I actually felt very bad about it all.

Ideally we would like an ornamental tile detail on the hanging tiles but they are £785 per 1,000 which is out of our budget and a bit of a shame.

We looked into getting Professional Plumbing Services to do our plumbing. They were recommended by Nu Heat and sent along their quote in a very posh-looking folder. I'm sure they would do a very professional job but their quote was astronomical.

15th December. Clear night, new moon and stars.

A good night for the flaming torchlight carol-singing procession around the village. It was really magical. Afterwards we had mulled wine and mince pies at the village hall while Richard Ingrams read the last chapter of *A Christmas Carol* with the village children sitting around the Christmas tree.

17th December

We have finished stage 2 of the build and need the money released for stage 3. I spoke to Sharon at Buildstore who said it was being processed and we should have the money by next Tuesday.

January 2008

Mr Clark has finished his contract with Lloyds TSB, and found another one with a company in Newbury called Telekinesis.

The rain comes in and the building is like a two-tiered swimming pool. I have to sluice it all out every day and try to make sure that no one is standing under the stair hole, so I holler, 'Look out below!' If they haven't heard it's tough luck I'm afraid. The carpenters have made gashes and cuts in the protective plastic film which covers the floor, so I have had to tape them all up with a little help from the Pickle on one of her after-school visits. It is moisture-proof but this is deluge proportions.

JJN Roofing are very straightforward to deal with and are checking the quantities we need for the hanging tiles. Like Malcolm from BLR Roofing, they also said to go for Clayhall tiles as they really can't see the difference between them and the handmade Heritage Medium tiles. I compared the two and I see what they mean and they are a lot cheaper.

All is well, so I ordered the tiles. What a relief.

Darren says we need soakers, not troughs, for the Velux windows. I have no idea what this means. I hope it becomes apparent.

Boge, the painting and decorating marvel, will get all the paint for us from Dulux as he gets a trade discount.

The skip company will charge us £5 a day if we go over our 14-day limit, so we'll get it taken away ASAP.

To do:

- Paint stuff
- Buy Velux windows and flashing kits
- Chase up plumbers
- Buy ironmongery for all doors

We'll have to locate the bath at the other end of the bathroom as there is now a chimney in the way due to architect error, so we won't be able to fix a shower in the bath because it is under the slanting roof. Mr Clark is not at all happy about this, but there is nothing we can do about it now.

The ceilings upstairs will be lowered slightly to allow for more loft space. We can then do away with the collar beams, apparently.

It's really dark and gloomy, so we bought some £5 floodlights from Screwfix.

Top tip* Don't hire lights – buy them as it works out a lot cheaper.

I also bought myself some skiing salopettes in Oxfam which are the bee's knees. No more builder's bum for me, they're really snug. I'd recommend these for any site manager.

Due to being outside in the weather all day, when I get indoors of an evening I have a burning complexion as though someone has given me a good slapping round the chops. To remedy this I did try slathering my face with Vaseline in the mornings to see if it would help, but by the end of the day I just looked like a sticky-faced miner.

Sometimes I go round to my friend Debbie's house for a warm-up, a cuppa and a good old goss. She has *Vogue* magazine. Sometimes I go to my friend Jo's. She's got an AGA. It's a real bonus for me to have great friends in the village (with lovely warm houses) who are prepared to listen to me banging on about the build.

I feel a bit embarrassed really but the other evening my feet swelled up and wouldn't go down. I ran them under the cold tap and put them up in the air but to no avail. I got really panicky so Mr Clark rang NHS Direct who got a doctor to ring back. He made me answer all sorts of questions and told me that it would be ok and the swelling should go down soon. He said I had just been on my feet for too long and basically to keep calm and literally cool. So I watched the *Ten O'clock News* with my feet up and wafted them around. Huw Edwards is always so reassuring. I love Huw. I get so worried about him when he is reporting from a war zone. I wonder how Mrs Huw feels.

The Jeld-Wen window frames are in. Caversham Glass will come next week to glaze us. I can't wait. Mr Clark has made frames out of battens on which we stretched plastic sheeting and then put up to temporarily fill the window openings in the oak frame. I apparently wasn't impressed enough with the frames. I actually was but it is really tricky keeping up the enthusiasm when you're knackered and cold. We had previously put a tarpaulin over the front but it flapped about too much and kept the neighbours awake. Our poor long-suffering neighbours. We've put plastic over all the other window openings. I love my staple gun. I love my husband too, so I have decided not to do any more jobs with him.

Kieran is putting vertical battens on the roof. He's using special fixings which have a thread but no head, made by Helifix, which are apparently the thing to use. They are very expensive and of course not in the quote. He keeps running out so I begrudgingly trundle off to get some more. Getting hold of them is tricky as I have taken up everybody's supply already. It's getting to be a bit of a joke and I can't help feeling he is taking the piss somewhat.

11th January. Rain all day.

Today is the last day for Bob the carpenter. The carpenters soldiered on through the rain. They told me that the scaffolding isn't right and hasn't been right all the way through, and now they are nearly finished. I ask you. How can I be a proper site manager if no one complains? It's a health and safety nightmare. Hell no – it's more than that. It's a conspiracy. Paranoia, that's what it is.

I rang the scaffolding company to ask them to put it right and they sent a chap along while I wasn't on-site. The chap told Kieran that they would be back to do the remedial work at some point. I then gave the scaffolding company a call to arrange a suitable time for them to do the work. They told me that they thought the scaffolding was in actual fact all there and the carpenters must have moved it around. They also had the cheek to say that Kieran had said that we didn't need them to come back. I got quite annoyed at that point and, channelling my best Margot Leadbetter, told them that it did indeed need finishing and that I would expect them back ASAP. They will be back next Tuesday or Wednesday.

I must make sure they bring us a proper ladder and they don't charge us extra. The one they have given us is very wobbly and not tall enough.

The scaffolding was found to have bits missing after all.

The house is now mostly silver due to the Celotex insulation boards, like a big angular spaceship.

We'll have to decide on the staircase soon. It would be great if we could get one off the peg as it would save us a load of money. If that is the case we think the bottom step might have to be slightly shorter than the rest, as the insulation and screed in the floor will be put in at a specified height.

To do:

- Electrical connection
- Staircase
- Make a list of questions for Martin Jackson (BBS)
- Exterior doors
- Blinds for the Velux windows
- Towel rails

Adam from Peppard Building Supplies has found us the front door we wanted. What a great chap. Now we need a stable door for the other front door. We've got two front doors, aren't we posh? We'll see what he can find.

Chas Crocker is making our oak window frames in Essex.

All the roofing materials are here. I expect Darren will be delayed by the rain.

12th January

The house is full of water, so I sluiced it out and had a tidy-up.

Our background ventilation calculation, according to the building inspector, is 90,000mm^2. The clever Mr Clark, however, has recalculated it as 70,000mm^2, and in that case we will only need three airbricks. I'm glad he is so good at sums. It's astounding how they make you build an airtight house and then make you put holes in it for ventilation. Mad. Although actually it is quite sensible to have some air coming in if you have an extractor fan – you wouldn't want to suffocate while you were making the dinner if you had your boiler, wood burner and extractor all going at the same time I suppose. Thinking about it, I am thankful we will have our air bricks and vents.

To do:

• Ducting from the air bricks to the vent holes behind the stoves
• Rockwool insulation
• Order Ashbury Multi tiles – to get here by the end of next week

Mr Clark has put down a deposit on the Olivieri boiler which we're buying from Stoves Online. We must make sure we get a manual for it.

We have found a plumber. Mr Clark isn't sure about him but his quote was good. He said he can do a couple of days the week after next and then we will try to get a schedule out of him. He suggested that we buy a shower which is easy to get parts for. Very sensible.

I must do a critical path. My wipeable wall calendar now has coloured stickers too. No one is sticking to my schedule, however, but we're getting it done nonetheless. The house is house-shaped, that's the main thing.

To do:

- Get lead for flashings
- Get a ton bag of sand and a bag of cement and plasticiser for Darren

Top tip* Use plasticiser in your cement for finishing off jobs as then it won't crack and fall off.

It's a right faff getting the stage completion certificate done so we can get our stage payments. In theory the paperwork should run nicely from one lot to another, but it always seems to get stuck somewhere along the way and I have to ring all of them to make sure they have sent it off.

BBS (the building inspector) send an instruction to Self-Build Zone to issue our stage completion certificate. Self-Build Zone then send the certificate to Buildstore who in turn instruct the Skipton to release the money. We then sign a stage release form stating the stage we are at and send it to Buildstore. Easy. Apparently not. Buildstore have two offices. The form gets sent to their office in Scotland and they then send it to their other office in Swindon where it gets stuck in the mailroom for days and days. Our contact at Buildstore left without letting us know and now we are buffeted between three or four of them. Self-Build Zone always deny any knowledge of instructions from BBS and so it goes on and I grow another grey hair.

A new search on the land has to be carried out by the solicitor as time has run out. This is apparently necessary to protect us from any unforeseen conditions that could affect our property.

Tim Charman and his chum from Southern Electric came along. They gave me a scare by saying that in order to connect our electricity to the house they would have to dig up the road and it would cost us tons of money. I was mystified and asked them if we couldn't just have the cable put in a trench from the pole in the garden to the house. This confusion went on for about half an hour and my brow was getting most furrowed. Luckily it turned out to be one of those wrong-end-of-the-stick conversations. He had thought that I wanted the overhead cable moved and put underground. I have no idea why. As it turns out we can just dig the trench and he will bring us some cable. Phew.

27ᵗʰ January. Sunny and quite mild.

The snowdrops are out.

Mysteries (who does what and when?):

- Guttering
- Screed
- Insulation
- Plasterboard and OSB (Oriented Strand Board to put behind the plasterboard)
- Hearthstones
- Trench for the mains electric cable
- Corners on vertical fixings for tile battens (as Kieran hasn't done them)
- Gaps around the windows
- Plastering

Top tip* Don't put a roll of lead behind your car seat and put the brakes on hard.

The Nu Heat delivery time is approximately three to four days, five at most. The water tank they are supplying is a thermal store cylinder made by EnergyMaster, which means we can hook it up to various sorts of energy-generating systems.

February 2008

The termites, or electricians as otherwise known, have started. They proudly announced that they never do their own clearing up on-site. I'm not impressed.

Top tip* Take photos of where the electrical cables are for future reference.

The soakaway that was made has already silted up so we need another rainwater pipe.

Chas and his mate fitted our rather handsome oak door and window frames which, as Kevin might say, 'communicate their presence with a strong but silent beauty,' and now Chas is going off to Thailand, lucky bugger.

I love the smell of the oak. I think they should bottle it and sell it as perfume. I'd dab it behind Mr Clark's ears.

We had to buy some six inch nails, as the roof battens that Kieran had put on were very wobbly even with the expensive Helifix fixings which he insisted on having. So Darren went round hammering the nails into them. Mr Clark built vertical corner battens for the hanging tiles as Kieran obviously didn't realise that you can't fix things to fresh air.

Darren advised us to get the TV aerial on now to save them damaging the roof tiles. Very sensible but now the whole village is taking the piss.

Darren has started the roof with his labourer Liam. They covered the whole thing with Tyvek Supro, nailed on the battens and are now getting on with the tiling. The singing is pretty loud and the words to songs on the radio get changed, so I am very glad that Margaret is a bit hard of hearing. Liam turned up on the first day with trainers on and his jeans trailing in the mud, so Darren bought him a pair of boots. Liam has to go off to do his community service every now and then. He doesn't want to tell me what he did to deserve it and I don't really want to know. He has a certain youthful charm but also the ability to wind Darren up. When Darren has had enough, he comes and sits in the shed with me and bends my ear until he has calmed down enough to carry on. He's doing Liam a huge favour by taking him on. Liam really doesn't give a toss. He doesn't realise what an opportunity he's getting to learn an excellent trade. I think Darren's patience will run out soon.

I'm living on Cup-a-Soup and chocolate biscuits. Darren's packed lunch is very well ordered and neat and makes me envious. I had my very first Pot Noodle this week, which I have to say was actually quite nice. I had been putting it off since my hung-over friend Zoe had come to the site for a visit and brought a couple with her. Not being hungry at the time I had put it in the mouse-proof container for emergency provisions. I never thought I would do it. I'm a Pot Noodle slag, or maybe actually just a lapsed Pot Noodle snob.

Darren chats up all the passing horsey ladies and he's getting quite well known now. He also keeps me going with his cheeriness. Mr Clark takes the mickey and says that I love Darren. It's true I do love Darren. He is keeping me sane. Apparently he goes ballroom dancing to keep Mrs Darren happy and so they can spend some quality time together. I am trying to imagine him doing the rumba.

Liam saw his first pheasant the other day. He said, 'What's that? Is it a cat?' We pointed out that cats don't have feathers. He now thinks he's David Attenborough.

We are very nearly watertight. All the Jeld-Wen windows have been glazed and the roof is looking magnificent. Toby, Mr Clark's friend and demon biscuit-eater has, put the Velux windows in. I expect Kevin would be pleased that these will 'create an abundance of natural light' in the upper rooms, and I am sure he would be most impressed by our architect's decision to put one in the sloping ceiling of the landing, which now beams a very useful stream of light down the stairwell.

I am trying to get used to the fact that I'm not able to step through the window apertures as a way in from the scaffolding any more.

To do:

• Get ventilation tiles and adaptors for the roof. (These are special roof tiles that act as hidden outlets for the bathroom extractor fans and vent pipes)

I have to make sure the orange fencing is over the driveway all the time now, as there is no way I want Brian wandering on-site. A couple of times he has sneaked in and scared the bejesus out of the carpenters by creeping up behind them. I have to be extra vigilant as he is getting worse.

I drop him off and collect him from his day centre on a Thursday and take him for a coffee and cake in the garden centre café. He observes things very loudly now and reads out the signs and the blackboard menu in the café. Unfortunately if he sees anything unusual he makes his observations with even more gusto. We were driving over Goring bridge with the windows down as it was an unseasonably sunny day when he said very loudly, 'A FAT WOMAN WALKING A DOG!' Alzheimer's is an awful thing. He gets very upset if we don't go exactly the same way home each time, as I learnt to my peril. He gets very stressed if he thinks I might miss a turning. He reads all the signs along the way every time, not missing any. We go past some fields on the way home and he always says, 'Look at that view – isn't it lovely?' Sometimes we sing songs on the way home.

He likes to make me laugh too and makes some great faces and often gives me a wink. Margaret says he only winks at people he likes. I am honoured.

Margaret says that he is not the man she married. He doesn't know who she is sometimes. Apparently they were going somewhere in the car the other day and he said, 'You would have thought Margaret would have come along wouldn't you?' 'Who do you think I am then?' said Margaret. It must be really upsetting. He goes to a group for people with dementia called 'Singing for the Brain', which is run by the Pickle's Grandma in Tilehurst. It's a great opportunity for him to sing because he enjoys it so much. He belts it out with immense enthusiasm, as I found out after standing next to him at the Christmas church service. It puts me off as it is rarely in tune, or in time, but he loves it. Mr Clark and I sit towards the end of the pew with him in the middle, in order to block his way so that he doesn't wander off.

Waldemar and his Polish team will come and render the dormers next week.

We found an innovative rendering system from a company called Lime Technologies in Abingdon. We'll be using lightweight 25mm Hereklith boards which are made from strands of wood fibre and wool and are glued together with a substance called Magnabond. Apparently the boards have both good thermal and sound insulating qualities. Once these have been tacked on, you trowel on a layer of render 3–5mm thick. This is combed through with a brush and a layer of glass fibre reinforcing mesh is put onto the joins where there is risk of cracking. This is left to dry; 1mm of render supposedly taking one day to dry. Then you put on another layer of render to finish it off, which should give you a total thickness of 33mm. In all we have around 30 square metres to cover.

The Polish will be doing the tacking too and they will put the Rockwool insulation in as they go. We'll have OSB behind quite a lot of the plasterboard for fixing cupboards and shelves onto.

Top tip* Make a note of which walls have OSB behind them and which haven't to prevent disastrous cupboard failure. It hurts if you have a *cupboard fall on you, as I found out to my dismay when I was about 18. I was felled by a cupboard that had flown off a wall and was pinned to the fridge where I was found covered in tomato sauce and lentils.*

At last we have a Jewson account. Better late than never. We'd been forgotten about, and there were no reps to be seen even though we'd put in a request. Up until now we'd been getting all of our materials from Peppard Building Supplies. Apparently Adam from Peppard has just had a heart attack and is off work. I always ask for him when I call them as he is an old friend and sorts things out for us. It is a bit of a shock as he is younger than me. I hope he's ok.

Mandy, my namesake, is our contact at Jewson. She is quite fearsome and smells of fags but I really like her. She is sending me brochures by the dozen. We have some good chats, not really about building though. There aren't many ladies in the building trade, so I was heartened to see a lady manager at the Newbury branch of Jewson. I was concerned that, being a woman, I might not be taken seriously, but am pleasantly surprised that even though I stand at the counter at the builders' merchants and don't look entirely like I know what's what I don't get any comments, not to my face anyway (only when I'm taking an age choosing which colour bucket to buy). I look sufficiently grimy and dour which helps I think.

I'm getting much more confident on the phone with suppliers and tradesmen I've got the lingo and I've got a dictionary of building terms too, which we bought at the National Self Build & Renovation Centre in Swindon. I now know what a nogging is. I can't believe not many other people do (it is in fact a short horizontal piece of wood which fits between the vertical struts in your timber frame making it nice and strong). I just slip it into conversation and people are impressed and think I know what I'm talking about. There are a lot of abbreviations to get to grips with, but there I am talking about my DPC, my DPM and even my MDPE pipe as if I'd known about them all my life. Mr Clark is impressed. He bought me a box of Maltesers as a reward for being so clever.

Some nights though, when I shut the shed up and it's dark and cold, the bloody padlock won't close properly and the icy wind is giving me neuralgia, I get quite despondent and cry all the way home. I don't feel sorry for myself – it's just life at the coalface and I'm a knackered grubby labourer with responsibilities. It's quite hard to stick to a minimal budget and do as much as possible without paying someone else to do it. It would be impossible to have a paid labourer as work would be too sporadic and I have my standards. My site is well ordered: 'A tidy site is a happy site.' I spend all my time shifting things from one place to another.

Every day decisions have to be made and if I can't get hold of Mr Clark I have to make the decision myself and hope it is the right one. I have to weigh things up and tidy up, and I have to sweep. When I'm sweeping, annoyingly I sometimes get an irksome earworm stuck in my head. It can be a name, a phrase or a song, and it just goes on and on. The phrases are mostly building-related, 'air source heat pump, air source heat pump'; the names are really random, 'Kirstie Alley, Kirstie Alley, Kirstie Alley'. The worst one was when I got 'If you like Pina Coladas' stuck in my head for a whole week. Where do they all come from? Somewhere in the pleats of my mind I suppose. They must get released in times of stress.

My salopettes ripped when I bent down, much to the amusement of the roofers. I had to have a trip to Oxfam to buy some more. My new ones are stretchier and even more stylish. They're black with zips.

I am glossing fascias and soffits in between wintry showers. Tricky, but I've got to get it done before the scaffolding comes down. I love the scaffolding, although I have to be a bit careful not to knock my block off when I'm walking round corners. I've tried tying some red and white tape to the end of scaffold poles. It doesn't work that well, most times I try to wear my hard hat but it just falls off when I bend down, so I'm thinking of making a chinstrap. I wonder if Kevin discards his hard hat as soon as the cameras are turned off.

Up on the scaffolding is the only place you can get a phone signal and the views are amazing.

I bought some knee pads. Mr Clark asked me if I really needed them or could I do without. It seems that he doesn't care about my knees either. I told him that I had bought them already and they are staying on my knees, so there. Knee pads have made my life complete.

We now have a rainwater drain all the way down to the bottom of the garden.

There are currently three electricians on-site all getting on with it. I must ask them about a switch and light in the loft. We need a socket in the kitchen for the Olivieri pellet boiler.

To do:

• Tell Southern Electric that we would like the electricity supply connected to the house on 15th March

12th February. Sunny since last Sunday, so got a lot of painting done.

Liam buggered up part of a fascia board when he got in a strop cutting in around the dormers, so we're going to have to do some creative mending with some wood filler and glue. Luckily we have some fascia board left.

The Caversham Glass man came to measure the windows for the oak frames. He said he was in a rush as he had to go and visit a friend in Compton. I can only imagine it was a lady friend as he wasn't concentrating and didn't even do a template for the triangular top window. 'Hmm,' I thought, 'If that fits first time I'll eat my hard hat.'

18th February. Warm sunshine but freezing in the shade.

There have been frosts overnight which make me worry about the paintwork.

20th February. Cold but some sunshine; misty mornings.

A good stretch of dry weather for Darren. He has put the ventilation tiles on.

25th February

Eleven out of seventeen windows had to be redone. Even with a template the triangular glass wasn't that brilliant. I've seen this sort of thing on *Grand Designs* before. I think if I had a chance to rewind I would pay more and get a tip-top company to do the glazing. It didn't help that I had to go off to a funeral in the middle of it all and leave them to it.

Some of the glass couldn't be fitted into Chas's oak window frames as there was scaffolding sticking through the apertures.

Building a house is a mysterious thing if you've never done it before. Each day is a revelation. It is an adventure and a bit of a roller-coaster ride which has now gathered its own momentum.

Kevin would probably now ask us how the 'journey' is going for us. We would put on a brave smile for the cameras and tell him that it is 'awesome'. Which, despite everything, it is.

The fascia boards have all been glossed now and most of the soffits have been primed and undercoated.

Everyday life has to carry on too which is a bit of a pain. I'd like someone else to do the shopping, cooking, washing and cleaning but it all has to get done. We do have less washing at the moment though, as I wear site clothes most of the day and they don't come off until I hose myself down of an evening. Then it's straight into pyjama mode. There isn't much ironing, only Mr Clark's work clothes and he does those. But that's life, isn't it?

The electricians and plumber have finished their first fix. Mr Clark is still a bit worried about the plumber. You should have seen him putting in the pipes for the underfloor heating upstairs. He's a big bloke but disappeared from view in a wrestle with a load of huge spaghetti-like underfloor heating pipes. He doesn't inspire confidence.

Kieran came along and put 90mm Celotex insulation in the rafters. That should be snug. It is all getting much tidier and we are nearly ready for the plasterboard.

We're having Kieran trouble again. He said that he forgot to include the insulation for under the floor in his quote, even though his original quote says 'all insulation'. Is he trying to pull a fast one or is he just badly organised? We will give him the benefit of the doubt but feel that something strange is going on.

Once again it is that old conundrum, should we have bought all the insulation ourselves? Bit late now.

My poor weather-beaten face. Honestly I don't think it will ever be the same again.

28th February

The roof is finished. Martin Jackson from BBS said that it had been done really well. It looks magnificent. His only requirement now is that we put in the air vents next to the wood burner and the pellet boiler. He will send off the completion certificate so that we can get our next stage payment.

The underfloor heating will be put in downstairs when the walls have been plastered.

We now have a weatherproof house. This is a truly momentous day. Break out the bubbles.

March 2008

2nd March

Mother's Day.

I took the afternoon off. Had tea and biscuits with Mum, Margaret and Brian. I caught Brian feeding his chocolate biscuits to Tanzy. Margaret says Tanzy often feels off-colour and now we know why … chocolate biscuit poisoning.

To do:

- Buy OSB
- Order render
- Loft flooring
- Balustrades/bannisters/newel posts
- Fit front doors
- Buy locks and hinges for front doors

- Buy air bricks and ducting
- Trench for mains electric cable
- Extra underfloor clip track for downstairs underfloor heating (it needs to be fitted 50cm apart)
- Arrange screeding
- Get the shower and all bathroom stuff
- Buy towel rails
- Sort out drainage at front for the driveway
- Re-point brickwork
- Bathroom floor tiling
- Buy all internal doors

The Polish team are on-site. We have made a plan of works and Waldemar assures us that he will be on hand to instruct and translate at all times.

NB: For indoor plastering and rendering you need stop beads to make clean and precise corners, and for outside rendering you need stainless steel stop beads and also bellcast beads on the lower edges to deflect rainwater.

I asked Lime Technologies if they have instructions in Polish for putting the Hereklith board up. But no, they don't.

The Poles have rendered the dormers and put the rest of the Hereklith board up with a nail gun containing stainless steels nails. They are now plasterboarding which seems to be taking them a long time. There is a lot of standing about not doing very much. I was under the impression that they were going to be fast and efficient as I had heard so much about how good these gangs of Polish builders are. Even though my great-grandmother was Polish, I don't speak a word apart from having learnt herbata and czajnik, tea and kettle apparently. There is a lot of gesticulation and nodding which is making me anxious.

Despite being specifically told not to, the stupid buggers plasterboarded the kitchen fireplace, inside and out, when in fact it should be finished off with render, and to really piss us off had stuck it on with some very strong bonding stuff. As Waldemar had given them the schedule of works and instructions, I thought I could leave them to get on with it for a while. Bad move.

Mr Clark and I had a very fraught evening trying to pull it all off again before the bonding dried. Unfortunately some of it had already set quite hard and we had to get if off with a hammer and chisel. We were not best pleased.

It is all getting extremely stressful. Waldemar is hardly ever here and the Poles keep getting it wrong even though they nod and say 'yees yees' when they really don't know what I've asked them to do. I have to ring Waldemar all the time and as the phone signal is really dodgy it's quite a task. I'm pulling my hair out. Waldemar keeps assuring me it is all ok. I don't know if it is. Should I just get them to stop?

My alcohol consumption has risen somewhat.

Even Kevin would be worried now. This would probably feature in an earnest piece to camera just before the ad break: 'In building, like life in general, communication is essential. Without it things can quickly spiral out of control and a language barrier is just that – a barrier – a sometimes impenetrable wall between, in this case, client and builder. One can only hope this problem can be overcome so that the build continues according to plan and Mandy doesn't lose all her hair or blow the budget on Chardonnay.'

Clive came to take some of the branches off the ash tree so they don't damage the roof.

5th March. Sunny and showery.

It was a good job I didn't do any fascia board painting today. It would have been ruined.

The second lift of scaffolding has gone. It's looking good. Well, on the outside anyway.

I think I must be making grooves in the B4009 travelling to the site and back. My little Peugeot is doing well, although I did get a bump up the backside recently caused by a huge lorry which was coming round the corner towards me on my side of the road. The roads around here are narrow country lanes so I headed for the hedge. Unfortunately I had to stop or I would have been flattened. A white Transit van went up my backside, so to speak, as he was travelling too close behind me. It wasn't too bad, just some dents and my rear light was shattered. I was a bit shaken though. Our friend Mr Williams says you should always drive along country lanes as if there is a horse around every corner.

11th March. Squally showers, storms on the coasts.

12th March

Darren has fixed a leak from the chimney and in the downstairs loo which was full of water this morning. He has started battening ready for the hanging tiles, but might have to wait for better weather.

Brian escaped from the day centre in Wallingford. I saw him getting out of a car next door but didn't see who had brought him home. It is great that people are looking out for him.

The hanging tiles were delivered and Darren started putting them up. It was a nail-biting experience – if I had made the wrong choice it would have been dire. Luckily all was ok. There was a big difference in the colour from one pallet to the next but he mixed them up and it worked out pretty well. I had to change some of the tile-and-a-half and corner tiles as they were completely the wrong colour. I went back to JJN Roofing and they let me hand-pick the ones I wanted. Good people (apart from one of their drivers who called Margaret a silly old bag when she was being 'helpful' with his delivery parking).

At the weekend, the Klargester Biodisc arose from its earthy hole due to heavy rainfall and the fact that Mr Clark had pumped all the water out of it. Luckily none of the pipes broke. Nick and Ben have reinstated it using metal rods and extra concrete.

Darren will be finished by Friday. He says that he has never seen such a ropey tacking job. The electricians are annoyed because the Poles have used bonding stuff to fill in all the joins and cracks in the plasterboard, which has made their job of cutting out the holes for the sockets and switches really tricky. The wall next to where the stairs will be is banana-shaped. It seems they didn't put any noggins in to support the plasterboard, so it is all flapping about.

Luckily the Poles have gone home for two weeks, thank God for that.

The scaffolding is coming down next Tuesday. So we will have to organise a tower for the Poles (and some poles for the tower, ha ha). If they are allowed back on-site that is.

To do:

• Order the staircase and get it fitted
• Get underfloor heating done and pressure-tested
• Get the floor screeded
• Get door handles
• Plumb in the downstairs loo

I am now on the deeds.

26th March

The scaffolding was taken down today. It's a bit like getting the braces off your teeth. Now we can see the whole house it looks huge and is a feast for our tired and baggy eyes. I managed to get a coat of gloss on the window frames before the scaffolding was taken away. At last we can get the doors and windows in where the scaffolding was in the way.

After not much deliberation and me saying to Mr Clark in no uncertain terms, 'I'm not having those bloody Poles on-site again,' we have decided to sack this particular bunch of Eastern Europeans as they really don't know what they are doing and we can't trust them. We have also decided not to pay them the final amount outstanding and may even ask for some money back to put things right. I think we have learned the hard way. It's all about saving money you see. It is getting very boring as all our conversations end up with those miserable Poles. We've had to ban Polish talk, especially at dinner time, as it puts me right off my food.

We have now recruited a chippie called Frank and he is putting in the door linings and window boards (for people who don't know, window boards are the same as window sills; it confused the hell out of us).

How much distance do you need to leave between the Celotex insulation and the downlights in order for them to be fireproof? Well, I can tell you. It's 50mm clearance, with a fireproof cover on the light.

NB: You have to put in a certain percentage of low-energy light fittings to fall into line with building regulations.

When we get the internal doors we must keep them lying flat until they are hung.

The electricity to the house will be connected on 18th April. The electric meter will now go in the cupboard which was originally for the heat pump.

To do:

- Get glass for stable door window
- Look at wooden flooring

Nails, nails everywhere. I just keep picking them up and Kieran keeps complaining about getting punctures, but I am doing my best. He's blaming the roofer, but did he not drop any at all himself?

I would have loved to, as Kevin might say on *Grand Designs*, 'lavish my attention on the craftsmanship and design' of our staircase, but instead I watched Kieran fix our £99 Jewson's off-the-peg staircase to the banana-shaped wall as best he could. I think we will have to do something creative – I don't know what – there's a gap of a couple of inches between the wall and the foot of the stairs, and about an inch at the top. I feel like I should have been more on the case at the time. If I had known they needed to put more noggings in, I would have made them put more noggings in. It is a big and harsh lesson. Waldemar had kept on assuring me he had it all in hand and 'don't to vorry'. I was wery vorried indeed.

Magically the staircase fitted perfectly lengthwise without alterations, which was some consolation.

April 2008

We called a meeting with Waldemar when he got back from Poland. We told him that we thought the work wasn't good enough and had to be put right. He looked like he was going to cry and put his head in his hands and said he was going to give up and go back to Poland. I wished he would. We told him that our decision was to use the money that we're not giving to him to get someone else to fix it.

A heated discussion was had. We wobbled the plasterboard that had no support behind it so that he could see it with his own eyes, but he was still adamant that it was ok. The gunk they had filled the joins and cracks in with was plasterboard bonding which he said 'vill nevcr crack', and demonstrated by poking it firmly, at which point it cracked loudly and he said, 'Oh … oh dear,' and had to concede defeat. He had no idea about noggings either. I ask you.

Frank has drawn anti-Polish slogans all over the walls. He says they all have heads like footballs and has done drawings to illustrate this. He is not happy, although he *is* happy to put the plasterboard right for a daily rate.

5th April. Snow.

I took photos of the house sitting in a pretty snowy scene; they'll do for the Christmas card. I'm very proud of what we have achieved so far.

I think I might have offended the Portaloo man. I'm not sure. His truck pulled up and I shouted, 'IT'S THE POO MAN' very loudly, and as it happened he was standing right next to the open window at which I was standing. 'Cup of tea?' I squeaked. 'Two sugars,' said the poo man. He came in and I offered him a biscuit and he sat and had a chat. Apparently he had recently split up with his girlfriend and he told me that there was some dispute about the house. They couldn't work out an amicable split, so he had driven a truck into the house and demolished a large part of it. 'Then neither one of us could have it,' he said. I hoped I had smoothed my faux pas over by the time he'd got through quarter of a packet of chocolate digestives. I was quite glad to have the electricians on-site.

I have been making videos of the progress of the build. I always take the same route. People can't watch it though as they say it makes them dizzy. I think my camera work needs some improvement. I wanted to keep a video diary but I don't seem to get time.

Nick and Ben dug a trench for the electric cable and have spread the leftover pea shingle all over the garden. It's all stuck together with mud and is now lying as a thick carpet everywhere. They said it will aerate the soil. It has aerated me I can tell you. Nick eventually scraped it up into a huge pile with the digger and I have done my arm in scraping up the rest of it with a spade. Kind Mr Clark helped me though. They say they will get it taken away.

I must say (excluding the pea shingle incident), Nick and Ben have done a very professional job. Maybe Nick has forgotten all about the roundabout days. If he does remember he hasn't mentioned it, thankfully, but is probably secretly glad that I don't smoke anymore.

Chas's window glazing bars are now going banana-shaped too. There seems to be a theme emerging here.

We've had our last stage payment now so we'll have to be extra careful with the budget.

The bags of plaster and stop beads are ready and waiting and I've masked off everything that needs to be masked off.

NB: If plaster gets on the oak, the oak will turn black. We got some marvellous sticky blue stuff on a roll from Screwfix to protect it.

The stairs have been carpeted in leftover Tyvek held down with staples. How I love Tyvek Supro – it has so many uses, you can use it over and over again. It is also waterproof which is an added bonus. You get 140 square metres per roll and it only costs £59.20.

Brian has had what remain of his teeth out and will be getting new dentures. I think the pain is bothering him a lot.

14th April. Unseasonably cold. Sleeting.

I showed Mum and Clive around the house and they were very impressed with being able to go upstairs.

We have recruited a plasterer who is a friend of Frank's and who I coincidentally went on a date with ten or so years ago. He took me to see *A Midsummer Night's Dream* in Oxford in the open-air theatre at Magdalen College. He was a much more cheery sort of chap back then and we had a really great evening, but he can't have liked me much as he didn't ask me out again.

He has been here for a week now and is halfway through plastering the main bedroom. We got off to a bad start. He arrived on-site in a stinking mood, scowling and moaning. Luckily his mate Frank was there to diffuse some of the gloom. I had a bit of a ding dong with both of them because they were going on and on about what wasn't right with the build and I am feeling sensitive and weary. The plasterer knew there was some making-good to do as we had been over what he had to do twice and I presumed he had allowed for it all in his quote, but apparently he hadn't accounted for this … or for that … The two of them got me more and more wound up until I could stand it no more and stomped off-site. I got into my car and fumed my way down to Goring. I was in the shop buying a cheese sandwich and some crisps to console myself, when I got a text message apology from them. They said that having a good old moan was just the way they got on with their day, so I texted them back and said that 'I could bloody well do without it'. It gives me heartburn. Mind you, that could also be due to the copious amounts of white wine I neck of an evening. My diet is appalling.

I keep urging the plasterer to employ a labourer to help him as he has got a bad back which is slowing him down. He's wearing a back brace for God's sake. We should really have got a gang of plasterers but the budget wouldn't allow. A big bonus of having him on-site is his little white dog, Molly, who comes with him. She is a sweetheart and cheers me right up, although she does make my trousers a bit muddy in her friendliness. Frank tries his hardest to keep his friend motivated and sets up boxes and boards to help him get up to the high bits. But it is to no avail. He is depressed and is a bottomless pit of sorrow. Perhaps he should stop smoking those funny cigarettes. Not even my stupid jokes or the chocolate and crisps I buy him help. Sometimes he downs tools and says he is going home. It's going so slowly it's like pulling teeth, but I have to say he's a very good plasterer and what he has done has been admired. I tell him so, fat lot of good that does me.

I think one of the trickiest things for me is having to navigate the battle of the trades. I didn't realise how sensitive these tradesmen are. You have to tread very carefully so as not to upset them. There is also the crossover situation. It is sometimes unclear whose job it is to finish off what. The ones who have just left are blamed by the incomers for doing a shoddy job and not leaving the site ready, so I am piggy-in-the-middle trying to get it all running seamlessly. Our seams are a bit wonky but I do the best I can to straighten them up.

16th April. Cold but with a bit of sunshine.

I took Mum to the John Radcliffe Hospital for a something-oscopy which, in her words, 'entails someone looking up one's arse with a camera and watching it on a TV screen'. While she was being filmed, I read a book on how to do tiling and also wrote a long to-do list. I managed to catch a sneaky forty winks too.

19th April. Grey, chilly, rain.

When the plastering has been done in the main bedroom we can get the ensuite bathroom floor tiled.

Southern Electric have connected the electrics to the house and Mr Clark has filled in the trench. Oh how he wishes he had a digger. He wants one for his own.

22nd April. Warm with a chilly breeze.

The ceiling downstairs is being double-tacked and noggings are being put in everywhere. The whole house is stuck together with Gripfill adhesive and is nice and sturdy now. Frank is a cheery soul and his English is perfect (he's from South Oxfordshire). He's a bit bonkers though and threatened to kill one of the electricians. It's all ok now, which is good because I'm not sure the insurance would cover that sort of thing. To be fair, we had spent a whole afternoon measuring out where the ceiling light holes had originally been before they'd been covered up through retacking. The electricians had come in with their plan the next day and ignored all our hard work. We were both a bit peeved.

The electricians forgot to make holes for the downlights in the main bathroom but say they will put them in.

Frank has been using his artistic skills on the walls again to portray the Poles on crucifixes, all with downturned mouths, and has written slogans that I shouldn't repeat. I'd better not tell him about my Polish ancestry.

I've got OOS (Occupational Overuse Syndrome to you) in my arm; I also have a lot of DUTN (Dust Up The Nose). Plaster dust dries your skin up, makes your hair brittle and gives you dry brown bogeys. I look like that woman off *Terrahawks*.

The plasterer is working in the main bathroom now. The main bedroom and ensuite bathroom are finished.

I've tried to make the plasterboard as ready as I can, sanding and making sure the screws aren't sticking out. Apparently it isn't good enough.

The stairs are creaking.

Bleak days.

Frank says that the electricians are ATGNI (All The Gear, No Idea). I think they are a breath of fresh air actually.

To do:

- Measure for slate tiles for the bathrooms
- Measure for the wood flooring
- Put the front (stable door) on
- Re-varnish the other front door
- Mask off the Glulam beams ready for painting the ceiling
- Keyhole covers for doors
- Buy loft hatch
- Make outside cupboard doors

Mr Clark has made a splendid job of rerouting the vent pipe in the bathroom. The plumber had installed a 100mm pipe which would have meant a load of awkward boxing-in. We replaced it with a 50mm pipe which fits snugly behind the plasterboard.

Frank has cut the loft hatch hole to the right size. Now to get a loft ladder.

To do:

- Downstairs loo cupboard
- Tile bathroom floors
- Ducting for air vents
- Air bricks
- Hearthstones
- Check availability of bathroom stuff
- Put door handles and window catches on

Eeyore the plasterer is plodding on.

Frank is putting the front doors on; he's a fantastic chippie and a manic, joyful bundle of energy and enthusiasm who really lifts my spirits. He's made us an under-stairs cupboard which will be most useful and will hide the underfloor heating manifold. We just need to get weather bars and glass for the stable door now. Frank says he finds it difficult to stay focused and organised. I suggested to him that he should buy a notebook and write everything down, and that way he wouldn't have pockets full of bits of paper and forget things that he should remember. He bought himself one and says it's working so far. I couldn't do without my notebook.

I wonder how many miles of masking tape I've used so far.

Top tip* Don't leave masking tape on windows for too long or it is a real bugger to get off.

Mr Clark went to buy the loft ladder and I went to Wallingford Glass to order the stable door window.

I gave Kieran a photo cube with pictures of him and his chaps building the timber frame. He was surprised but I think he liked it.

May 2008

9th May

My lovely little Granny's birthday. If she was alive today she would be 107. I still miss her. I don't do any knitting since she died as I have no one to get me out of trouble if I get in a mess. She would have thought Mr Clark was a lovely boy. It is a shame they didn't meet each other.

Mr Clark and I have just got back from Lulworth Cove where we went for a much needed short break.

15th May. Cold and grey.

I've got the lurgy, horrible hormones and a very slow miserable plasterer.

19th May

My birthday. Mr Clark bought me a Huw Edwards T-shirt. I am very pleased.

Now the plaster is dry upstairs I have managed to get quite a lot of painting done indoors.

Top tip* I was advised by Boge the decorating genius to apply a watered-down coat of emulsion first when you are painting new plaster and then you can put on subsequent coats.

It's amazing what a difference it makes. I like the pink plaster look and also the smell, which I imagine is something like being in a giant clay pot, but it's fantastic how solid the paint makes the rooms feel. I've got a painting hat with a peak which stops the paint splatting in my eyes. I learned a harsh lesson, and that is, if you are painting Glulam preserver on your Glulam beams and you are looking up and press hard on your brush, you are likely to get an eyeful of the stuff.

Top tip* Wear goggles if you are decorating while looking up.

Peeling the plaster-covered plastic from the floor is very satisfying. You end up with beautifully clean boarding and the dust is no more. Until of course your husband comes and does a bit of sanding or the electricians bore more holes. I borrowed Margaret's old hoover. It looked sort of pre-war and she said she didn't mind it getting mucky. It was working ok until it went bang and caught fire. Mr Clark's mum has lent us her Henry who doesn't suck much up but is very welcome nonetheless. I would like to buy one of those powerful hoovers that builders have; Mr Clark wouldn't.

I was going to tile the bathroom floors myself but I bottled out when I met a hairy tiler in the tile shop and told him of my plan to use slate. He looked earnestly at me and shook his head at the very idea. He said that laying slate is very tricky. So we asked Mr Williams, our friend from the village, if he would do it for us. He did a great job as he is a clever soul, very calm and most meticulous. It has been great to have a good influence on-site; he has helped to make the atmosphere much more relaxed. Now we can get the bathroom stuff in, hurrah.

Frank has put together all the oak stair parts. It looks great and now we won't break our necks. The components are manufactured by a company called Richard Burbidge who let you order however many spindles and newel posts you need for your staircase, and provide lengths of base rail and handrail to make up your balustrade kit.

We'll get some money back on the roof tiles that we didn't use. Raven Roofing, who supplied the Ashbury Multi tiles, have picked them up and will send us a cheque. They charge for picking them up however.

Brian went missing in Wallingford while Margaret wasn't looking. She rang a friend who lives in Wallingford who came to help her look for him, and Margaret went to the police station. The police eventually found him in Waitrose with a large Toblerone up his jumper. He wasn't made to give it back. Margaret explained to the Waitrose manager about Brian's Alzheimer's and he was very understanding. Margaret paid for the Toblerone and said if it happened again she would pay for any inadvertently purloined items.

Brian likes to keep a supply of sweets and apparently hides them all around the house. He pockets them from the sweet stall at the Saturday Market in the village hall. Margaret reimburses them regularly and happily they are very understanding.

June 2008

3rd June. Monsoon rain and very chilly.

Mr Clark's birthday.

8th June. Lovely sunny day.

The discs in the Klargester are now merrily turning around; I must go and christen it. I had such a problem with getting help from Klargester when we put the motor in and the pump didn't work.

In my experience you shouldn't take advice on the phone from young ladies who don't know what they are talking about. To try and sort out the problem I rang Klargester and the young lady I spoke to told me that I should submerse the motor under water. I asked her if she meant the pump, so she went off and asked someone else in the office about the problem and assured me that it was the motor that should be submersed. I didn't do as she advised. What is wrong with these people? Eventually

I rang the chap who sold us the Klargester. He had left but his replacement, a very sensible fellow, thought that the float must be stuck and suggested that I poke about a bit and give it a wiggle. It worked like magic and the float came up and the pump pumped.

It does worry me. Sometimes when you ring a building supplier you get a really inexperienced young person just saying whatever comes into their silly heads. They just make it up as they go along. One of them said to me, 'What's a stop bead?' I ask you. I'm usually already annoyed because I've been half an hour trying to get a signal on my mobile and I would be balancing on one leg up a step ladder which is most tricky on a windy day. It gets mighty windy up here as we're on top of a hill. Once when I was up the scaffolding on my stepladder, a huge gust of wind blew and as I toppled over, I had to hang onto a scaffold pole for dear life and ended up Wallace and Gromit-style, flapping like a flag on a flag pole.

I got pipped to the post. Frank the chippie had christened the bathroom toilet already, a number two as well. We had to re-jig the soil pipe arrangement from the loo as the boxing-in of the pipes wouldn't have worked otherwise. I think our plumber just wants to do the minimum he can for the money as every connection to every loo and sink is leaking. I accidentally turned the tap on while the pipe was disconnected and Frank got poo water all over him, at least it was his own.

Top tip* When buying toilets, get ones with big apertures to accommodate number twos. If the holes are too small you will end up cleaning the toilet ALL the time. (Now we know why they were cheap.)

We went to the reclamation yard to look for some bricks for the garden wall. While Mr Clark looked for some suitable bricks I did some scouting about and found some quarry tiles which might do for the kitchen floor. The lady who owns the yard is an amazing woman – Amazonian in stature with an enormous bosom, very pink lipstick and bleached blonde hair. She knows her stuff and can carry any weight you'd care to lumber her with. She is very impressive and I am in awe of her. Her husband also works there; he has a gold tooth, a gold chain around his neck and a round tum. But his wife is the boss.

18th June. A chilly easterly wind has given way to wet westerly winds, strong and blustery with some sunshine.

19th June. Strong cold wind but with blue sky and warm sun.

We have to move into the house in six weeks' time, so we must keep going even though we're really tired. We are having to dig deep for seams of untapped energy. There must be some in there somewhere.

The ground floor insulation is in and the plastic membrane and underfloor heating pipes have been laid. It looks like a huge blue swimming pool.

The floor screed was pumped in and levelled out in a very professional manner by the muscular Troy and his Polish labourer. I was a little worried that we had a Pole on-site; I kept my distance and gave him a hard stare every now and then. We've got quick-drying screed.

As a rule normal screed takes one day for every millimetre in drying time.

Top tip* To test whether your screed is dry enough to lay flooring, you get a piece of plastic about a metre square and stick it to the floor with some gaffer tape, leave overnight and have a look under it in the morning. If it is dry you can then lay your floor.

We have ordered the wood flooring for the dining room/sun room and hallway, but are wondering whether it would be best to stick the wood flooring down or have a floating floor. I think we should go for the latter option to allow expansion when the underfloor heating is on.

NB: A floating floor is when an underlay is put down with the floorboards sitting on top, not actually floating you see.

The rest of the bathroom stuff is here now, apart from the shower door.

The electricians have done the distribution board and we have a double socket indoors. What luxury. Get the kettle on.

To do:

- Order wood pellets
- Get Olivieri boiler
- Contact BT
- Look at carpets

NB: The carpets have to be of a certain tog value, like a duvet, but the lower the tog value the better it is at letting heat through. This ensures that you get the best use out of your underfloor heating. The best flooring for underfloor heating is stone.

To do:

- Taps for sinks
- Doormat
- Box in bathroom pipes
- Put oak beading around door
- Skirting boards and architrave, door jams and doors
- Guttering and downpipes
- Tiles for shower and bathroom
- Get more paint

Kieran the carpenter had assured us that he had got the front door height right and had left enough space at the bottom for the screed. It was a good job we reduced the thickness of the screed because otherwise it would have been spilling out of the door. Now we have no room for a doormat unless it's 2mm thick. We could dig out a small foot well but that could be dodgy because of the underfloor heating pipes.

Priorities:

- Hearthstones
- Garden gate

Sean the plasterer came along today to start on the outside render. We didn't have the right beading so he faffed about a bit and then went away again. I spent all afternoon searching for 10mm stainless steel stop bead. I had to drive the Monkey wagon as my car was out of action. Actually it doesn't say Pick up Monkeys on the side of the van any more. It says 'ick up Mon ey' on one side and 'Pic p onkeys' on the other. The Ikea delivery business is no more – I think Mr Clark has enough on his plate as it is. It was a bit scary to drive as it is so big.

Top tip* Sometimes you might need EML (Expanded Metal Lath – ie, mesh) for your rendering needs. It hurts, a lot, as it is really sharp so don't try to cut it without gloves on.

23rd June

The fireplaces have been rendered; the plastering is finished and grumpy has gone. The whole place is breathing a sigh of relief. I rang the loo-hire people and said that they can take the Turdis away now that we have a flushing loo or two. The water is on and all we have to do now is get the boiler.

July 2008

The Turdis has gone. Maybe to Gallifrey, who knows?

Yesterday I got a call from Alison, a neighbour who recently moved away. She had spotted Brian in Blewbury out on his own. I had borrowed Margaret's phone as we hadn't got ours connected yet, and she was calling to find out if Margaret wanted Brian to be brought home. So I rushed next door and told Margaret, who went straight off to collect him. I called Alison back to tell her that Margaret was on her way and she said she would try to keep him occupied until he was picked up. He must've walked for miles over the Ridgeway that afternoon. His walking is his medication. He must have very strong walking muscles by now.

Mr Clark has been doing some research on tracking devices for Brian so that we can keep an eye on where he goes. Ellie, Brian and Margaret's current social worker, who is turning out to be a star, is looking into the funding to get him a really good one. She is moving on soon though and Margaret is worried who she might get next, as she says that Ellie is really on the ball and a complete contrast to the social worker they had before. I suppose it's the luck of the draw.

Mr and Mrs Clark senior have moved out of the family home where they have been living for forty-odd years and have moved into a flat in Tilehurst. It's a really great flat and is nice and big, but it's a bit odd for everybody.

3rd July

The oak flooring is down. A couple of cheery chaps came along and did a fine job. It has made the whole place look bigger. It's good we didn't go for wood in the kitchen too, otherwise it would've looked a bit too much like a village hall.

To do:

- Register the house with West Berks Council
- Get newel caps
- Airing cupboard door
- Garden wall
- Garden gate

8th July. Weather not too bad but still a cold wind.

I keep having dreams about Jeremy Clarkson. It is very disturbing.

Priorities:

- Taps
- Tiles for shower

Still no Sean as it is a bit showery. Mr Clark is getting uppity about him as am I.

We have run out of money and so will have to try and borrow more funds from the Skipton. We have put in a request.

I bought some doormats, a broom and a loo brush with the Homebase voucher I was given on my birthday by my brother Paul and his girlfriend Tania.

The quarry tiles for the kitchen floor have arrived and I've scrubbed and scrubbed them as they had gone a bit green from being kept outside. The hearthstones have been ordered from Stone Circle. At their business HQ they have huge and impressive slabs of marble. When I build a house on a big budget that's what I'll have. Some of it is really beautiful. Dream on. Anyway we got some pieces of bargain-basement green Cumbrian slate offcuts which will be cut to the right size with vent holes in the appropriate places.

Where would I be without my knee pads.

13th July. Blue sky, white fluffy clouds.

I took my mum on the Chinnor to Princes Risborough steam train for a cream tea as a late birthday treat. We spent a superior and very enjoyable afternoon together. The window by our seat was misted up so we didn't get to see much of the view. We were too interested in stuffing our faces anyway, so it didn't matter much.

14th July. Sunny. Warm outside but chilly inside.

Am very happy because Mr Clark will be on-site for the next three weeks.

BT have put a phone line in.

I painted the living room and the downstairs loo while my friend Camilla painted the lobby.

H came along and we laid the higgledy-piggledy kitchen floor. He was cursing because the tiles weren't all exactly the same size. I said it would give the floor charm and character; he said it would look a right bloody mess and buggered off, leaving me to do all the grouting. The whole house is a bit wonky which is surprising really as it's all new. At least the smaller tiles we got for the lobby and the loo are all the same size and the floor is nice and flat due to the muscular Troy and his laser level. It was a bit stressful for H cutting the smaller tiles on the tile cutter as they kept on breaking. I'll have to go back to the reclamation yard for a few more.

Grouting is exhausting.

H has lent us his tower to do the outside rendering. The weather is bad so there is still no Sean. He says we are messing him about; we say we don't have a direct line to the great weatherman in the sky.

I must say I am impressed with BT who have now called twice to see if our new line is ok.

Mr Clark and I laid the hearthstones in the kitchen and made a thoroughly good job of it, what a team. We wrote our names in Gripfill – 'John 4 Mandy' – and stuck the stones on top. I grouted them and now they are ready for the Olivieri pellet boiler which will be with us on Monday.

All the flexible pipes the plumber has put in are leaking. He says he hasn't used them before. Nice of him to use us as guinea pigs. The taps on the bath have been put on wonky and I'm a bit worried about straightening them up in case it causes more leaks. He has also put the thermal store tank round the wrong way so now we won't be able to get any doors on the airing cupboard. It'll have to be moved.

We've discovered that our thermal store tank doesn't actually have a facility for us to connect to solar panels. Oh for God's sake.

I am really in love with the house now and find it hard to go home at night. I can't wait to move in.

We stayed the night on Saturday. We slept on the futon that Mr Clark's friend Dobbo had given us. It was great to be there but I got a bit too overjoyed with it all and drank far too much wine. We had been invited to a friend's house for breakfast in the morning. I didn't make it, but Mr Clark couldn't resist the lure of bacon. He left me nursing my hangover and hiding from the sunlight which flooded through the bedroom windows.

18th July

The electricians have put in some sockets and all the doors are on.

To register the house we have to have a house name.

The West Berks Council lady said it will take a couple of weeks to process the registration.

Decorating schedule:

- Take masking tape off Glulam beams
- Do another coat of paint on walls
- Do all glossing
- Tile shower

To do:

- Order shower doors
- Order carpets
- Finish skirting and architraves

We got a bargain sink. Mr Clark's mum has an OAP card which she can use at Focus and she gets a good percentage off. It was already marked down too. What a result.

The electricians have inherited the electrics for the heating system as we are not letting the plumber anywhere near it. They won't be able to do the lights for another couple of weeks but have wired up the cooker and cooker hood.

21st July. Summer, lovely and warm but a bit breezy.

Mr Clark is using his time off work to get his teeth stuck into the skirting boards and architraves. He is also painting ceilings, which is very good of him as my neck hurts. We've now got a coat of paint on all the walls and he has made an outside cupboard door for the wood pellet store. He looks like a different man now and is enjoying being on-site doing his thing. It is a real joy to see him happy. I have put some custard creams in the biscuit tin, so that will make him even happier.

Luckily we have got the extra money from the Skipton so we can get finished.

The plumber will come in the day after he gets back from his stag weekend. We're hoping he'll be finished soon. It's a bit inconsiderate of him to get married in the middle of it all. Sean still hasn't been and is now going on holiday.

Talking of weddings, some friends from the village were getting married last weekend and I didn't want to miss them coming out of the church. I decided that as soon as I heard the church bells I would rush down from the scaffolding and run to the church to catch a look at them before they went off to the reception. I got a few choice looks from the wedding guests as I arrived wearing my grubby boiler suit and a dust mask on my bird's nest hair. I am imagining the wedding photos and people wondering who the small blonde grubby builder is in the background. I hope when all this is done I don't discover that underneath the builder's dust and muck all that is left is a wrinkly old leather bag of a woman.

Mr Clark is still putting his woodwork 'O' level to good use and Frank the chippie is putting the internal doors on. 'Dordogne Oak' from Howdens are rather good and give the impression that they are made of solid oak, but are in fact veneered chipboard. They look quite posh and are nice and heavy too.

We got our first load of wood pellets today in 100 plastic bags. Overloaded and spilling out all over the place.

We have chosen the hardware for the oak doors and windows in a brushed steel effect. I got most of them at Drews the Ironmongers but had to get the window furniture from a small shop in Reading called Knobs R Us or something.

Nick has built half of the garden wall between us and Margaret. It's quite nice actually as we can lean on it and have a chat, like in *Hector's House* and just like proper neighbours, but up a ladder. Margaret is pleased because as she says not many people get to choose their neighbours. I hope we live up to her expectations.

So many thunderbugs. I've painted quite a few into the ceilings but I reckon I'll have to stop until they've gone. They are so itchy, they're driving me mad.

I am feeling a bit overwhelmed.

The electricians have put some more sockets in.

To do:

- Make a structure for the kitchen sink to sit in
- Tile the shower
- Choose carpets
- Get shower enclosure
- Get oak floor edging strips

For the completion certificate we will need:

- Electrical certification
- Boiler certification
- SAP calculation
- Air test

The Olivieri wood pellet boiler has arrived. Mr Clark and our friend Mr Williams ingeniously rolled all 250kg of it in with two metal cylinders, much like the method people must have employed getting the stones from Wales to Stonehenge. A much shorter distance though, just across the floor from the back door.

There has been quite a problem getting the right size flue pipes and connectors for the boiler. Mr Clark eventually sorted it all out with Philip at Stoves Online.

I noticed the plumber looking at some instructions today. That's a first. He was scratching his head and rubbing his chin – not a good sign. He is, however, the only one who can install the Olivieri.

Hopefully he will have finished the water tank and immersion heater connections before he goes off to get married. On

Wednesday he was nearly a goner. One of the electricians came in through the front door with a funny look on his face shaking his head and looking a bit pale. He was muttering under his breath, 'Here but for the grace of God'. I wasn't sure what he meant but he then beckoned to me to go and have a look in the outside cupboard, the one with the downstairs loo the other side. He had been working on the back wall of the cupboard which is where the electricity meter is located, and had looked on in disbelief when he saw a drill bit come through the wall millimetres away from the main electric supply cable. The plumber had drilled his hole for the waste pipe 7 millimetres away from certain death. What a plonker. At least he didn't die in our downstairs toilet.

Top tip* When you are drilling through a wall, if you can get to it, take a minute to have a look at what is on the other side.

The connections the plumber has made to the water tank are leaking, and now he has one day to fix them, and put in the downstairs loo and the kitchen sink. I feel bad for him as he is actually a really nice bloke and I'm glad he didn't die. I just think his mind wasn't on the job. He was concentrating on selling a house and getting married. To his credit though he did install the boiler ok, but blotted his copy book once more by sticking the flue parts together with extremely strong glue, so when we wanted to get the cap off the bottom to give it a clean we couldn't. Unfortunately it's a bit mangled now.

The electricians feel a bit guilty about recommending him, so they did a lot of work for us this week. All the sockets work. The week after next they will put all the downlights in.

Mr Clark has made a fantastic structure for the kitchen sink. It's quite rustic and is made out of fence posts and odd bits of wood. I don't know what we will do for a kitchen, they're so expensive. I think we'll have to go shabby chic, a bit like Mr Clark.

A chap from Howdens came along and measured up for one of their kitchens which are decent enough but a bit plastic-looking and still out of our price range. He created a visual on his computer, which is really interesting as now we can see what it could look like. A friend has suggested I go to auctions to get the kitchen stuff and then we could have more of an eclectic look.

We now have hot water. What joy. We have a kitchen sink too. The plumber has gone off to Mexico on his honeymoon, so fingers crossed there are no more leaks. He said to me that he reckons he has gone from zero to hero now … We'll see.

Mr Clark installed the cooker hood and I put my sticky finger marks all over it. We will have to make a vent hole in the outside wall for the extractor fan. We've changed our minds about where the kitchen sink will go. It is now going next to the big window, so that we can nosey out of it at people walking down the road while we're doing the washing-up.

The Pickle has made a stage out of delivery pallets and is making us endure instalments of her own invention which she calls *The Funny Show*. Mr Clark is allowed to pick her up from school once a week and she comes here for tea. She comes every second Sunday now too.

One of the better *Funny Show* jokes:

Why did the toilet roll roll down the hill?
To get to the bottom of course, silly.

I reconfigured the site office so as to accommodate the wood pellets.

One of the young lads in the village is very enterprising and keeps coming round to the house to ask if there are jobs he can do for a bit of pocket money. I can give him small jobs now that it isn't a proper building site. He is very money-orientated for one so young and complained that his sister always gets more presents than him on birthdays and Christmas. I, up on my high horse, told him that he was actually very lucky to get anything at all and that in my day all I got for Christmas was a lolly and a satsuma. He is making a camp with his mate in the bushes up the road so I have given him some tiles and odd bits of wood to help with their build. He says they make a camp every year and then destroy it at the end of summer. Sounds like fun to me. I have been invited to have a look.

We have made signs to put around the village at strategic positions to try and stop Brian walking on the main road as it is really a bit dicey. The signs say 'Brian, this way', with an arrow pointing him along a safe route. Everyone in the village is looking out for him. It is really heartening for Margaret to feel that a community can support a person with Alzheimer's and can understand and accept the ways in which they behave. They are both loved and respected in the village so it is easy.

22nd–29th July. Heatwave.

Am STILL painting ceilings. It's taking an age because I have to neaten it up around all the beams. It has been so hot and I'm in the rafters. I'm in a terrible mood.

August 2008

7th August. Fresher weather after thunderstorms.

9th August. Grey, chilly and wet.

I threw a wobbler yesterday. I had spent a long time and numerous sleepless nights working out that we would paint all the walls white. Dulux White Cotton to be exact, with Brilliant White ceilings. We needed one more tin of White Cotton to finish off the decorating. Mr Clark was in full money-saving mode and instructed me to just 'buy a cheap pot of white paint'. I don't know what happened really, I lost it completely and kicked my handbag across the room and everything flew out. My poor mum, Margaret and her friend Andrea had come to help us clean the windows and were treated to a full-on tantrum. I think I was just tired. Margaret disappeared off next door, came back again and pressed £30 into my hand and told me I should go and buy the paint I wanted. Marvellous Margaret.

As Sean has disappeared, the not-so-cheery plasterer came back to do the rest of the lime render outside. He was really difficult to communicate with and started splashing render all over the hanging tiles. I asked him to wash it off before it dried which led to a bit of a contretemps, so he went off in a huff. I don't think he'll be back. Good. Mr Clark witnessed the scene, so now he knows what I went through for seven long weeks.

To do:

- Ring Bathroom Warehouse and get shower doors
- Get carpets
- Oak finishing strips and beading
- Spotlights for upstairs
- Matting for hallway
- Get bath panel
- Put kitchen door on
- Airing cupboard shelves and doors
- Hearth in sitting room
- Under-stairs cupboard
- Grilles for hearth in kitchen
- Go to tip
- Driveway and drainage
- Render
- Outside lights

I've got a really bad neck and shoulder but am plodding on with the painting.

Mr Clark's skirting was giving him trouble but after he borrowed Frank's nail gun it all went swimmingly. Now Mr Clark wants his own nail gun. We have a lot to do before he goes back to work in a week. He has, however, put up the guttering and fixed the downpipes with his friend Toby. You can get some very posh guttering but ours is bog-standard black plastic. Nothing wrong with that.

It's a bit stressful as we have to move out of our place in Bradfield very soon because someone is moving in. As long as we have finished the painting and the carpets are in we will be ok.

18th August

It has been great having Mr Clark here. He is not happy to be going back to work today.

Mr Clark's mate Dave Roper has built us a hearth out of bricks for our log burner to sit on. Dave was the bass player in 'The 'Deckchairs' which was the punk band that Mr Clark used to play guitar with when he was young and skinny. In fact that was how I first set eyes on my future husband. It was at the Purple Turtle Bar in Reading in 1987. They were playing there and I remember spying a homemade rocket in the air tied to a piece of string ready to fly over the stage, and some scruffy oiks looking all cool smoking fags doing their soundcheck. I was in an all-girl band at the time called 'Valley of the Dolls'. It took another 16 years for us to get together.

The electricians did a lot of scratching of heads trying to work out the heating system. A few calls to Nu Heat later and they managed to get it sorted out.

The carpets have been chosen and will be laid by Keith and Arthur the carpet fitters. I must clear all the rooms ready for their arrival. We must pack up our things in Bradfield too.

22nd August. Warm, sunshine, no rain.

Mum helped me pack clothes and do some cleaning at the house in Bradfield. I wiped off all the mosquito splats on our bedroom ceiling and gave it a coat of paint.

Part 3

Homeward bound

24ᵗʰ August

Final packing-up day in Bradfield. Mr Clark's mum ironed Barbara's washed curtains and Mr Clark and the Pickle cleaned the windows.

Who knew we had so much stuff? I'm so tired I think I'm going to keel over. The 'ick up mon ey' van proved very useful and we managed to move all of our things into our new house with a little help from our friends.

25ᵗʰ August. Warm day.

Bank holiday.

We're in! Exhausted but very happy to be sitting here in our box-filled, curtainless, unfinished home. The bedroom carpets look so sumptuous and luxurious I just want to roll all over them naked.

Still so much to do. Everyone has commented on how much they admire our sitting room hearth; the one that is made of bricks and cost practically nothing in materials. Not the Cumbrian green slate one in the kitchen which cost loads and is much more stylish.

Electrics to do:

• Light switch in lobby area for garden room
• Sockets behind TV
• Low-energy bulbs for the kitchen

- Heating electrics
- Dimmers for bedrooms
- Sockets for Internet and TV upstairs
- Outside lights
- Extractor in kitchen
- Narnia lamp post
- Move toilet light switch?
- Washing machine switch
- Bathroom mirror light

The plumber came along and gave us some more leaks, broke a panel on the wood pellet boiler and plumbed in the washing machine.

We've now got a posh mirror with integrated lights for the bathroom. I like it very much because it is quite bright and gives out a nice flat light which in turn whites out the wrinkles. I fiddled around with the bulbs using half energy-saving ones which are very white, and half non-energy-saving which are yellower. I think I got the ratio just right for the most flattering glow.

Mr Clark's rustic garden table has had a few coats of varnish and its legs painted, and is now our kitchen table. His sister Jane has given us six pine chairs and a cupboard/dresser so we have somewhere to eat and somewhere to put things. Dad and Sue have given us a small pine table with a couple of drawers which we are using for cutlery and as a work surface.

We have discovered that our Olivieri wood pellet boiler has vital parts missing. It seems also that the importers no longer import these particular boilers, so it might be difficult getting parts. All the instructions are in Italian. Everyone at Stoves Online is on holiday. Mr Clark is not happy about that and still not happy to be back at work.

Nick has gone on holiday, leaving us with a massive muddy puddle and a half-built wall. He promises he will get the drainage done when he gets back.

Waiting for the electricians to return. We seem to have been relegated to the bottom of the pile.

My body doesn't work anymore, my hands have seized up and I'm hobbling around like a hundred-year-old. I am so tired I think I am going to die.

No curtains yet. It's all very bright because we painted everything white. I have to go around the house with sunglasses on. (Nothing to do with a hangover, no.)

To inform:

- Doctors
- Banks
- Vodafone
- HMRC
- Car insurance
- Optician
- Dentist

The carpet fitters have fitted the stair, landing and spare room carpets now. It is a beautiful shade of blue and looks very tasteful with the oak stair parts.

The chaos is getting more organised. Stuff, stuff everywhere and where is the house build phone book?

We went to Country Stoves in Cookham to pick up our wood burner. Mr Clark has opted for a Clearview Pioneer 400 stove. It will give out more than enough heat for our sitting room but should we have gone for the optional boiler attachment too?

To do:

- Get flue for Clearview stove
- Install Clearview stove
- Redirection of post
- Slats for the airing cupboard

- Boards for loft
- Doors for airing cupboard
- Curtains, poles and blinds

Don't mention the plastic store Mr Clark bought from B&Q for the wood pellets. He hates its wonky ways with a passion.

No movement on the boiler as yet. We will have to make a fuss – we've given them enough time now. The Stoves Online chap who sold it to us can't get hold of the people who originally imported the boiler.

I have made a rather fetching pebble border in the shower made out of some slate pebbles that Mr Clark and I pilfered from the Jurassic Coast on our last trip to Dorset. I have sealed them so they should be ok. Now we just have to put the shower doors on.

The very young and good-looking plasterers Craig and Russell have been employed to finish off the outside render. I found them advertised in our local magazine. How I wish I had found them earlier.

We were given too much MC55 render. Lime Technologies say they will take it back and give us our money back less 15%, which I think is a bit cheeky as they were the ones who calculated how much we would need.

The electricians are finally here to sort out the sockets and switches. The cloakroom door is now hinged on the opposite side and has to open outwards due to its size and because of the sloping ceiling. It'll make a big mess if we change the switch to the other side of the door or to a light pull inside, so we're leaving it where it is. We'll have to get used to it.

The Olivieri boiler parts are on their way, apparently.

I stayed in all day waiting for the Olivieri parts and they didn't come.

Mr Clark put the flue together for the wood-burning stove and has sprayed it with black flue spray. When the fumes have died down we will be nice and warm.

The Olivieri stuff turned up; the replacement tile they sent was broken and the firebox had been used and was bent. We aren't happy. The importers of the boiler appear to be a bunch of monkeys. It turns out we have been fobbed off with an old model which doesn't have a pull-out ash box as was shown in the manual; this caused some confusion as we couldn't see how the ash could be emptied. Poor John from Stoves Online is dismayed and will try to sort it out. That is the trouble with having too many people in the chain. In an ideal world going straight to the manufacturer would be the best thing to do.

My arm is a nightmare – it's even painful to write. I should rest it but there is so much more to do.

Nick and Ben came and did the rest of the drainage at the front of the drive and have levelled out the driveway with scalpings. Now we must get some topsoil for what will be the lawn and some gravel for the drive and out the back.

You might think that we would be jumping up and down with joy to have moved in, but from the time you get up in the morning until the time you go to bed, walking around the house is quite stressful because all you see is what needs finishing.

Top tip* Remember to seal up each and every hole in your newly built house or you might get a mouse in the walls. Ours came in through a small slot in the brickwork under a window frame and then squeezed its way through a tiny gap where the ceiling meets the oak screen and Glulam beam. I heard it go plop onto the floor in the night and scurry off, never to be seen again.

We've decided to get the ensuite bathroom and sitting room

totally finished first, as they are nearly there anyway. Mr Clark is very pleased with his low-level blue lights which he can have on when he is showering. He got the idea when he visited the barn conversion where he'd seen the ground source heating, as they had them in their bathroom. It is quite an odd sensation when you come out of the shower having had the blue lights on – everything looks very strange and slightly surreal for a while.

Curtains are really expensive and I can't find any affordable ones I like. I have extravagant taste you see, a big-budget mentality and a little-budget reality. Mr Clark says I am being too fussy. I'm no good at shopping. It makes me despondent.

September 2008

Brian has got his tracking device and it works really well. It transmits the same way as a mobile phone and you can easily track him on a map on the computer. It shows the regular routes that he takes too. Margaret just has to remember to charge up the battery every night.

Yesterday we were looking at Brian's tracker and we saw that he was in the garden of a big house in the village. I got a bit worried as it looked as if he was actually inside the house, although he was probably just peering in the windows but we didn't know if the people who lived there knew about him. It was pouring with rain so Margaret got in her car and drove up to gate of the house, and Mr Clark hoofed over to have a look for him. After a bit of a search he found Brian just coming out of the garden; it seemed no one was any the wiser.

19th September

We went to see the importers of our temperamental wood pellet boiler, down in Devon. Poor Mr Clark has had a very stressful time trying to find out how it all works. At one point he got so frustrated, I was afraid he was going to smash it up and all we would be left with is £4,000-worth of twisted metal. I made him promise to walk away if it was imminent and smash something less valuable.

The people there were very rude and unhelpful. We were met in complete silence by the stony-faced Colin and young engineer Katrina, which made for an uncomfortable start. Colin, in a very unfriendly manner, intimated that we hadn't had a suitable person to install the boiler. Mr Clark informed him that in fact our plumber was a member of the Institute of Plumbers and Corgi-registered (stick that up your flue pipe you bugger).

Colin then said that access for repairs and servicing would be a problem with the space available in the alcove around our boiler, and pointed out that we have less than the recommended space at the sides, which in fact then made the warranty invalid. Mr Clark went completely silent at this point and got that pointy look in his eyes. I was a bit worried as he looked like he was going to give the chap a flying punch, but he managed somehow to contain himself and said that Stoves Online had assured us when we bought the boiler that we had adequate space around it. (So sod right off you arse.) Colin said that they wouldn't fix the boiler but would send someone to commission it for £290. It was agreed that Stoves Online should be asked to pay for the commissioning, as apparently they had bought it from someone who had bought it from the importers. Who knows what it had been through before it came to us.

They didn't have a record of our Olivieri being fired up and tested when it was with them after having been imported from Italy. Not very impressive.

Katrina took us off at that point and showed us how to fix an electrical connection in the boiler that should have already been connected, or must have come adrift in its travels. She then went off to their farm to get us some extra tiles. (They farm these things?) This was actually very decent of them, probably only done to appease the seething Mr Clark and avoid fisticuffs.

Mr Clark's parting shot was to say that he would be writing a piece for *Homebuilding & Renovating Magazine*, who would no doubt be very interested to know all about it. Touché.

The plumber will be coming soon to get the underfloor heating working. Am trying not to worry.

I spoke to Chas Crocker who will make us a kitchen worktop out of oak and then we can get the cupboards when funds allow. Mr Clark isn't as keen as me on the idea of an eclectic-style kitchen.

Clever Mr Clark has made more use of his woodwork 'O' level and has built a beautiful bookcase in the sitting room. We bought a couple of chunky Ikea shelves too, so now we can unpack some books and CDs. Happily the Billy bookcase, which we brought with us from Bradfield, is now stacked with glasses and fits snugly into the space just by the stair-cupboard.

We have discovered that we really should have made more provision for storage cupboards and will have to build them in at some point. We don't even own a wardrobe at the moment. We had a canvas one at N° 4 but it has been wrecked in the move. Our neighbours have kindly lent us their adjustable clothes rack for now.

We have officially run out of money. Mr Clark has had to cash in his Premium Bonds.

The house is still full of stuff that should be in the shed, but the shed is full.

To do:

- Doormat
- Felt for table feet
- Curtains and curtain poles
- Letterbox

- House name sign
- Get drive done
- Loo roll holders
- Bathroom cabinet
- Tiles for bathroom
- Get doorstep done

The Klargester keeps on tripping the downstairs ring, electrically I mean. I called the electrician who said that the Klargester needs its own circuit. The electrics keep going bang whenever we turn the underfloor heating on.

Both ankles are bad now and my tennis elbow isn't good at all. I can't even lift the phone to my ear.

I rang Frank and he said that he can come and do the airing cupboard slats and doors next week. I have done him a drawing with measurements. We really didn't want any MDF in the house at all. However, the stair treads are MDF and now these doors will have to be made out of it too as it is cheap.

Some things you have to compromise on. Some things you can't and shouldn't. I suspect Kevin would agree.

I sent an email to Chas with dimensions for the oak kitchen worktop.

I have got an appointment with the physiotherapist at Wallingford Community Hospital on 4th November.

Nick and Ben have finished the garden wall and gate. We've got a wooden gate between us and Margaret which we won't lock.

Nick has given us his whopping bill. Phew. We're prompt payers though. I know what it is like to be self-employed and to be held up by the selfish buggers who don't pay up and ruin your cash flow.

We have our SAP calculations from Shore Engineering and because our calculations are so good we don't need an air test.

The saga of the boiler and heating goes on.

To do:

• Order 10 tons of scalpings for the drive

It turned out that the electricians had wired the thermostats wrong as they hadn't looked at the Nu Heat instructions. So the mystery of the blowing fuses has been solved.

The plumber has had to fix quite a spectacular leak under the bath, which has ruined my paintwork in the kitchen. He also hasn't put any scale inhibitor in the underfloor heating pipes. We need this put in to protect the pipes from a build-up of limescale, as we are in a hard water area. It also protects the thermal store water tank from furring up. The underfloor heating is working downstairs but not upstairs as yet.

Mr Clark is as temperamental as the Olivieri boiler is proving to be. It still has to be commissioned properly and we need a lesson on how it works. We're hoping that this will do the trick as we have to babysit it all the time at the moment.

Having gone through a stage of not liking the house any more, Mr Clark and I both now love it.

Chas came and fitted our stylish oak worktop. It has made all the difference. Apparently we have to Danish Oil it six more times.

Mr Clark's sister Catherine has made us a beautiful ceramic house sign in green with cream-coloured lettering saying

'PEAR TREE COTTAGE' with dark etchings of pears and leaves. She's so clever.

November 2008

10th November. Rain.

Yesterday there was another flood. Luckily it didn't come in the house but it swamped the garden and the drive. The Klargester stayed put and thankfully didn't get flooded. Phew. I sandbagged the house air vents just in case.

We have asked West Berks Council if anything can be done about the slope of the road and the storm drains.

The plumber has finished his job, hallelujah. He has put some scale inhibitor in the underfloor heating pipes and now we are very warm. A bit too warm actually – we have been stripping off our clothes. I'm very glad we had underfloor heating upstairs as well as downstairs as the heat doesn't really rise. Well, it rises to just about halfway up the stairs and that's it. I suppose it's down to all that insulation and the double plasterboard between floors.

I was a bit dismayed to see a load of tannin from the oak sills outside streaking down our pristine new render in the rain. There's so much rain. I don't like it, it makes my hair go curly. Mr Clark says he likes it curly but I think I look like a frizzy mad woman.

December 2008

Mr Clark has had a tidy outside and it's looking a little less pikey.

Still waiting for the boiler to be commissioned.

My arm is just too bad now, so Boge came to finish off the decorating for us. I put Planet Rock on the radio to keep him company. All we need to do now is varnish the doors and balustrades and Mr Clark says he will do that.

The Olivieri boiler has been commissioned by the lovely Katrina from the impertinent importers. We now have an official boiler commissioning certificate. It is still a bit temperamental, however. It went poouff the other day and sent burning embers exploding out of the closed door. Someone told us we might need an air regulator in the flue. We still need those chimney cowls – I often see the pesky jackdaws peering into next door's chimney pots.

Christmas Schmistmas.

It's always a bit tricky this time of year as Mr Clark doesn't get to see his little Pickle on Christmas Day anymore and this always lends a sad air to the festive season. He used to go round to see her on Christmas morning to hand over her presents just like my dad used to do for me and my siblings when we were little, but now the Pickle's mum has decided that he's no longer allowed inside their house.

I have fond memories of Boxing Day at my dad and Sue's with those brilliant indoor fireworks that made worms when you put a match to them and the magic flower tree that grew when you put it in a glass of water. Oh how I loved the 1970s. *The Generation Game*, *The Wombles*, Donny Osmond, Big Daddy, Dr Who and my purple elephant-cord trouser suit. My brother in his space suit with his rocket launcher in the snow, and my sister in her orange hotpants kissing her Marc Bolan posters.

I wonder what the Pickle's fond memories will be. I know one of them will be Harry Potter. Unfortunately she talks all the way through the DVDs and tells us what's about to happen next. She can't help it because she knows them off by heart.

January 2009

My sister Kate and her husband Dave have been over from New Zealand and we have had lots of laughs and many drinks. Dave is a chef so is always handy to have around, especially at Christmas. He used to work for Led Zeppelin in the 70s and has some tasty tales to tell. We say he should write them all down because the world needs to know. He says he's not sure that the world is ready for that sort of thing.

My sis is a designer and one of those ever so clever people who are annoyingly good at everything. She designed and made us a mosaic for the bathroom. It's a wave pattern that surrounds the bath and carries on along the wall. Now I feel like a mermaid splashing around in the waves whenever I have a bath. I love it. It's made up of beautiful shades of blue and stone colours. It was finished off with only moments to spare. Dave was roped in to help finish the grouting because they were racing against the clock, as they still had a load of packing to do before heading off back to the Antipodes that evening.

Bryan with a 'y' and Wendy his wife came for a visit along with Mr Clark's parents. I think he was suitably impressed with the house but still a bit sore about the lack of beams. We had tea and cake and watched Barrack Obama's inauguration speech.

February 2009

17th February

Mr Clark bought me a day at Nirvana Spa to soothe my painful body.

He has also put a bird nesting box on the ash tree; it will be great if we get the blue tits nesting in there as we will be able to see them doing their thing from our bedroom window.

27th February

Mr and Mrs Clark senior have moved to Wivenhoe in Essex. They have bought a beautiful flat next to the estuary, just down the road from Mr Clark's sister and her family. They say that they wish they had moved there years ago.

Brian has lost his tracking device. It was attached to his belt which he had taken off. We think he must have gone for a number two somewhere in the wilderness. We spent hours and hours looking for it. The battery had run out so unfortunately we couldn't track it.

March 2009

25th March

I resigned as secretary to the parochial church council.

27th March

I had an MRI scan. It was a scary experience, especially because I'm a bit claustrophobic. You can choose the music you listen to while you are in the tube, so I chose Sting as it reminds me of happy times with Mr Clark. In I went and on went the music and the MRI scanner, which sounded like road drills and hammering. The nurse used the intercom to see if I was ok. I was doing deep-breathing exercises and trying not to panic but said I was ok. She forgot to put the music back on so I spent the rest of the time listening to the drilling and banging, determined not to give in. I managed to get through it though and the upshot is I apparently have bulgy discs in my neck and an impingement in my shoulder which is affecting my ulnar nerve, which is the one that travels from your neck, through your shoulder and down your arm into your hand.

The aftermath of sweeping, scraping, sanding, lifting, lugging, dragging, grouting, painting and varnishing is really crap and I wish I hadn't done it. If we ever build another house, I'm not doing any of the physical work.

I have had to stop taking Brian to and from the day centre now. He got really heated when he thought I might miss the turning for the garden centre and started bashing his fists on the dashboard of my car. I thought he might bash me next and that it could be really dangerous if I was driving. So I talked to Margaret about the situation; she understands completely and agreed that it might be best not to take him anymore.

Margaret doesn't rise early in the mornings and Brian does, so she keeps the doors locked and hides the keys until she has got up. This isn't working out as Brian just hammers on the doors trying to get out.

He now has two jolly ladies who come to the house to look after him. He escaped from them at the garden centre when they took him there for coffee and a cake. He is quick.

April 2009

Mr Clark rang HMRC National Advice Centre to confirm our build is a 'new build'. They said that according to section 4.1 of Public Notice 719 and the fact that we made use of only one façade of the original building, our house is indeed classed as a new build. Brilliant.

Mr Clark's bass-playing friend Dave Roper has been laying the Indian Sandstone patio and I have been cementing in some decorative patches of pebbles in the gaps. I'm afraid I had bad PMT and arm pain while he was here, which made me behave like a ratbag. I don't know Dave very well but I'm pretty sure he reckons Mr Clark has married a raving loony. The patio is looking lovely, however, and because the house is mostly open-plan downstairs with lots of full-length windows, it feels like the floor now extends to the outside. Kevin might say something like, 'The juxtaposition of the spaces creates a seductive and enduring communication,' and so it does.

16th April

Brian's behaviour is getting too much for the jolly ladies to handle now. They suggested that he should go to Prospect Park Hospital in Reading, which is a facility for people suffering with mental illness. Margaret has had to admit that he is getting too much even for her to cope with. She has been trying to get a doctor from the memory clinic to help but they have been very slow in responding. Along with all that and a complaint that Brian had exposed himself to some walkers up on the Ridgeway (probably while having a wee), she did as they suggested and he was booked into the hospital.

24 hours later Margaret was telephoned by the head honcho of the memory clinic, who is officially attached to the hospital, and informed that Brian had been sectioned. He said this was necessary because they couldn't keep him there against his will unless he was sectioned.

17th April

Margaret received a letter from the memory clinic doctor who she had been trying to get hold of previously, which said that he could come and see Brian. A bit late now.

Brian obviously wasn't happy at the hospital and walked and walked around the ward, shaking the doors and trying to get out, so they gave him drugs to calm him down.

Margaret and I were dismayed and in fact horrified when we went to visit Brian. He had fallen over and his eye and forehead were black and blue. He was hallucinating, and trying to pick things up that weren't there.

The falling over kept happening and every time we went in to see Brian he had new bruises. Margaret went to see him one day and said that she had found him sitting in a wheelchair looking like a zombie and talking gibberish. She said that she just stood there and burst into tears. Poor Margaret, poor Brian.

We told the nurses that a week earlier Brian had been out and about walking the Ridgeway. They thought that was impossible and said we must be lying. How bloody patronising can you get? I was incensed.

Margaret is beginning to realise the full implications of the section. It means that she has no rights over what happens to her husband from now on, and she wishes that she had been informed as to what would happen to him and what it would mean for her right from the start. If only that letter from the doctor had arrived a day earlier.

We went to a meeting with the head memory clinic doctor and his team to discuss Brian's care plan. Basically it was a discussion about what drugs to give him.

This is a list of the drugs they were giving him, obviously not all at the same time but they were trying him on different combinations.

Lorazepam
Seroquel
Trazodone
Olanzopine
Chloral Betaine
Citilopram
Zopiclone
Melatonin
Sodium Valproate
Paracetamol
Codeine Phosphate

We have discussions about breaking him out of that awful place, but we would only get arrested if we tried. He can't escape now; it's like a prison for him, with no fresh air and nothing to do.

29th April. Sunny and hot with big white fluffy clouds.

Swine flu is predicted and the media are scaring us into thinking it will be a pandemic. I can't get swine flu now, there's still too much to do.

May 2009

2nd May

Mum and Clive brought our pot plants and shrubs round so they could be installed on the smart new patio. She has been looking after them for us, so as payment I made a nice tea of Victoria sponge with real cream and a pot of Earl Grey. Mum took her dentures out to make the most of it.

I am doing research on hedging plants.

There is still a long to-do list and poor Mr Clark is having to work through it as my neck and arm are still rubbish.

Living in the house is great; leaving it is the problem. It is my baby. The pear tree is in blossom and I am so glad I saved it from those devil-may-care builders.

Sue, my stepmum, has very kindly given me a bit of money. Mr Clark and I spent it in Ikea and now have a stylish and comfortable new bed and bedding for the spare room. We still call it the Pickle's room just in case we can entice her to stay over again.

The fence ruined by the felled Leylandii tree has been repaired with some fencing given to us by our friend Frank Drew who has a whole heap of useful stuff in his garden. In fact his garden is mostly the heap of useful stuff.

7th May

Brian's first section has run out and he has been sectioned indefinitely under Section 3 of the Mental Health Act. This happened without Margaret's knowledge. Apparently they left a message on her answerphone while she was out walking Tanzy. I think it is very peculiar that they can inform someone of their loved one's sectioning on the phone, let alone an answerphone message.

8th May

Went to the 'Tour de Presteigne' electric bike event with Mr Clark and our friends Jo and Nick Williams. Velospeed Electric Bikes, which is Mr Clark and Mr Williams' new business venture, are touting their wares and joining in the race. They have imported some bikes from China but Mr Clark is very dubious about the quality of them. They are looking into getting better quality ebikes.

28th May. Lovely warm sunny day.

I went to my friend Camilla's hen party on a narrowboat on the Thames. This will be her third husband. The boat broke down at Culham but we had a really fun time even so. Mr Clark and the Pickle came to pick me up. She was quite amused to see one of her primary school teachers there with a nice big glass of wine in her hand.

June 2009

3rd June

Mr Clark's birthday. We went off to Hengistbury Head for the day.

8th June. Cold and windy.

I rang HMRC to see if we will get our invoices back when they have done with them. They said that they do in fact send them back.

11th June

We have sent off the VAT forms, receipts and the costs spread-sheet to Her Majesty's Revenue and Customs DIY Processing Team, 2 Broadway, Birmingham B15 1BG. I hope Her Majesty finds them interesting reading.

In Mr Clark's covering letter he asked them to note that the wording in our planning permission is a bit ambiguous. It might give the impression that it is a conversion of an existing building, but we have been assured that it is in fact classed as a new build. The only part of the building retained was the front wall and a small part of the façade. A new concrete raft was constructed to support the new walls.

16th June

Mr Clark received a letter back from a Mr Chrimes at HMRC to say that our application for a VAT refund under the DIY scheme had been rejected. This was because they believed our building to be a 'conversion of a residential garage occupied together with a dwelling'. In other words, garages are excluded from buildings that are treated as non-residential as they are considered to be part of a house. He returned all our documentation and said he was sorry that he was unable to give us a more favourable decision.

Oh shit.

It seems we have four options.

1. Write back to Mr Chrimes with any additional information
2. Ask for his decision to be reviewed by an HMRC officer not previously involved in the matter
3. Appeal to an independent tribunal
4. Accept the decision and that we won't get any money back

Poor Mr Clark is finding it all a bit stressful, what with the VAT and only having evenings and Saturdays to work on the house. The garden is still a building site but he has made a beautifully constructed raised vegetable bed out of the old rafters. I am so frustrated at not being able to do much because I'm in so much pain. My mum has had to take on a portrait commission for me because I just can't manage it at the moment. Clive has kindly said that he will come over and help out. Am going to see a neurologist next Tuesday. The Sauvignon Blanc seems to be the most useful medication at the moment.

Top tip* Don't overdo it if you aren't used to being a builder as you can damage yourself. If someone offers to help you lift something, LET THEM.

I've got to get a proper job now that we've got a huge mortgage. I've applied for loads but it seems that people who are overqualified are snapping them up and jobs are getting scarce. My choice of employment is quite limited now too as I'm not able to take on work which entails lifting or carrying.

I did get an interview at a local Steiner School as a teaching assistant. My nephew Eran goes to a Steiner school and I have been to a couple of his school fêtes before. The parents strike me as knitted, colourful and cheery types and I knew a bit about the Steiner philosophy, but I really didn't expect what was to come.

I was shown into the nursery by a woman who looked a bit Amish wearing an apron, where I was told to take off my shoes. I was then seated in an armchair and handed some wool to put in a ball because, she said, as I was observing I should have something to do as everyone had to be busy. 'Fair enough,' I thought. The idea is to make the school environment as much like the caring home environment as possible, and obviously at home parents would be busy doing household things. I was told I wasn't allowed to speak to the children.

I then went into another classroom where the children were doing art. 'Great,' I thought, 'I can obviously have a chat with them to see what they are up to.' But no, I was told not to talk to the children and not to share any opinions I had about their work. I didn't really see how this was possible as they had seated me at a table with a group of children all eager to show what they had done. Then I was made to peel carrots with the children in the nursery who all help to make lunch, still not allowed to speak.

I observed the class for which I would be teaching assistant if I was offered the job. This was easy as I sat at the back, so didn't need to take part at all. There was a lighting of a candle and a couple of bing bing bongs on a glockenspiel and some maths. There were only eight pupils in the class, all lovely and quiet and well behaved.

Lunchtime came and I sat with the children in the classroom while they had lunch. I tried not to talk. Then I was ushered outside. The children were curious of course and came up to talk to me, so I talked to them because if I ignored them, I thought they might think I was a bit of a weirdo. I was asked to water the vegetable garden and then taken inside again and told off for speaking to the children. I went to the loo at this point where I texted Mr Clark, 'Get me out of this God-forsaken hell hole!' He texted me back, 'Run away!' I thought it would be bad form to run away so decided to stay the course. After lunch I was made to lie down with the younger children for a rest and then listen to a story. After that I took myself off to my car as fast as my legs would carry me, frustrated and exhausted at not being able to talk, ALL DAY.

Weirdly, the teacher rang and offered me the job and I turned it down. I'm sure the Steiner way is a good way of teaching but I feel after that ordeal that it isn't for me. I told her that their interview technique was a bit strange and had completely put me off. She was very surprised. It is the polar opposite of George Palmer Primary School which is what I am used to. I like a bit of communication.

So now, in between writing job applications, I have somehow managed to be persuaded to be chairperson for our 'Parish Plan'. I am busily organising consultation events with the villagers and compiling a questionnaire. I've decided to run a film project with the young people in the parish as well. It'll be interesting to find out their opinions and see if they have any issues with life in the village – much less boring than a questionnaire. It's keeping me out of mischief, which is the main thing, but the trouble is people are avoiding me in the street now as they don't want to be roped into being on the steering committee. I don't really blame them.

Mr Clark is still working at Telekinesis. He hates it and is very unhappy. He hasn't been able to leave as the recession has set in and we still have so much to pay for, so for now he feels he has to stay there in his pit of boring IT hell. Happily though he thinks there isn't enough work coming in and they might have to let him go.

July 2009

16th July

We applied to the independent VAT tribunal to appeal Mr Chrimes' decision.

We've planted a vine where the old one used to be.

I sieved some stones out of the earth before we put the grass seed down for the lawn. My arm wasn't too painful which was good. I had been given a wrist support by the physiotherapist, which helped a bit. Mr Clark raked and tamped the ground down and then sowed the seed. It'll be a luxury to have a lawn. We pinned some weed-proof membrane onto the drive and out the back in the walled garden and covered it with wheelbarrow-loads of gravel. It's really taking shape now. Mr Clark dug out a semi-circular flower bed and I've arranged the remaining pebbles from the patio around it. We've inherited a large leafy fig tree whose fruit will keep us nice and regular, and I'm very much looking forward to a nice juicy pear or two. We bought a bird bath from the garden centre and Mr Clark's mum and dad's bench has been put next to the house under the overhang. We might build a pond as well, we'll see; but the rest of the garden will have to do as it wants for the moment.

The pigeons are pooing on the patio.

Brian fell badly due to a seizure and was whisked off to the Royal Berkshire Hospital. Margaret went straight to the hospital but couldn't locate him as he had been booked in under the wrong name, but she eventually found him. He had been put in a room on his own.

It seems that because of Prospect Park Hospital policy (due to the section) Margaret isn't allowed to be alone with Brian in his room at the Royal Berks. This is completely mad because he is so drugged up that he wouldn't be able to move about anyway, let alone be dangerous. Apparently there has to be a member of Prospect Park staff in the room at all times. Margaret complained and asked if they could sit just outside the door to give them some privacy. On one occasion this did actually happen, but wasn't permitted again, so as you can imagine communications totally broke down between Margaret, the authorities and staff put in place to make sure that the conditions of the section were carried out – with no exceptions. One particular day they sent a policeman to stand outside Brian's door in case Margaret got violent. Honestly, it was unbelievable. Can't they see that she is just very upset? Anyone would be. I know that she can hold her own but she really is tiny. How could she be a threat to anyone?

Margaret is traumatised. She thinks Brian is in a lot of pain and wants him to be examined properly, but she says that the doctors just dismiss her worries.

Ten days later Brian had an X-ray and was found to have a broken and dislocated shoulder. He must have been in a lot of pain but couldn't communicate it. The Prospect Park carers said that he had fallen when they got him to A&E after the seizure and it must have happened then. (Saves them a bit of awkward paperwork doesn't it?)

I found out that Margaret had been living on toast and marmalade. She is looking thinner but is eating more now thankfully.

Brian and Margaret don't have any children, although they do have three nieces who visit regularly. They used to come and stay a lot when they were children and played horses in the bit of garden that is now ours. It must have been strange for them when the land was sold but they have been really accepting of us and are glad that Margaret has neighbours who will look out for her. It is a mutual looking-after though. She looks out for us too.

Because people with Alzheimer's can forget how to use their bodies and Brian hasn't been out of bed for ages, it is now thought that he will never walk again. Even if he did get up, his arm is in a sling so his balance would be bad. The doctor said that he could be de-sectioned and returned to Margaret's care. She reckons that is a good idea and has a hospital bed coming which will be installed in their dining room.

Brian keeps spitting his false teeth out and because they end up on the floor they are now broken. Margaret has given up on them so he'll just have to do without. He spits his pills out too. He's still enjoying his food though.

At the hospital there is a bright, bubbly and ample-bosomed nurse who knows a bit about dementia and thought that she would have a go at getting Brian up and out of bed. Apparently she got him sitting up on the side of the bed, where he toppled face forward into her voluminous frontage. I can just imagine the scene. After that she got him standing, and the next time we visited he was standing up holding onto the window sill – it was like a miracle.

The delivery of the hospital bed has been cancelled.

It's all very well having a lovely oak gable-end window in your bedroom but how the hell are you supposed to get curtains to fit? We will have to find a solution soon. For now I have rigged up curtains using a broom handle and drawing pins. The ever-changing view of the fields through the seasons gives us a lot of pleasure but not at four in the morning when the light hits your eyes and wakes you up. The pigeons get up around this time too and do a song and tap dance routine on the roof. We had hoped that we would be more sound-proofed but there is no loft space above us, just a beautifully painted echoey apex with the Glulam beams.

We bought some marvellous Velux blinds for the Velux windows in the bedroom. There are two windows, one on the wall and one above it in the sloping ceiling, so we can lie in bed and look at the stars. How I love Velux blinds, they are such a brilliant design as they fit into the window unit itself and you can just slide them up and down. I was a design student once and really appreciate good design; I can get quite boring about it and once I see something ingenious I get quite excited. Mr Clark likes them and thinks they are very useful.

From the other window in the bedroom you can see the church in the distance. But can I find a blind I like? No I can't.

We've got a white slatted wooden blind on the ensuite bathroom window now. The view out the front looks over to our neighbour's paddocks. I love watching their horses, they have so much fun rolling around on their backs and cantering about and whispering in each other's ears.

I have never had a bedroom so big and I am loving it.

Brian is now walking about again and sometimes goes and sits at the nurses' station where he helps himself to their chocolates. Apparently he visits other patients in the ward too and removes things from their lockers. The doctor is making a plan to reduce Brian's medication, which is a good thing.

Mr Clark bought the Pickle a half-size acoustic guitar for her birthday as he would like her to follow in his guitar-playing footsteps. I don't think she's that interested, so I expect it will sit alongside my guitar gathering dust. My arm isn't good enough to play anymore and funnily enough I've lost interest too, which is a bit sad. My guitar has seen a bit of action in the past though. It played many gigs around the place, including the Marquee Club in London. It has been with me to Prague, busking with a cello player in 1994 (I got there before McDonald's) and to France for a little sojourn just before I met Mr Clark.

Luckily the guitars are quite ornamental; they hang around and fit in nicely with the artwork we have put in the sitting room. As we have a lot of artists in the family, we haven't had to buy any art. My dad is now mostly a sculptor and photographer and has given us some lovely pieces of his work. James Dodds, Mr Clark's sister's husband, is a well-known artist and has given us some of his linocut boat prints. My mum, being a painter, gets the full brunt of my pilfering. All I have to do is say to her, 'Ooh I really love that picture!' and she gives it to me.

I have put one of my own paintings of a raging sea at the top of the stairs which fills the space nicely.

We don't have the money to buy all the soft furnishings that I would really like. Curtains are still a big problem.

Mr and Mrs Clark senior have given us their big, beautiful, ornamental wall clock, and we have fixed it to the sitting room wall. Thank God we put OSB behind the plasterboard as it is really heavy and we don't want it falling on our heads. Unfortunately the tick is really loud and you can't hear the telly properly. This is particularly annoying during crucial bits of dialogue in *Midsomer Murders*, so we have stopped it for the time being. It is now permanently eleven minutes past one in our sitting room.

One visitor (I won't name names) came round, went into the sitting room, and said, 'Oh what a lovely snug'. She is right. It is snug but is in fact our only sitting room.

Margaret and I went to look around St Thomas' in Basingstoke, which is a residential home specialising in dementia care. It's part of the Barchester chain who, we understand, have a good reputation. The building used to be a convent and has corridors which link up to make a square, so when Brian is strong enough he will be able to walk as much as he wants. It has a big courtyard garden too so he can get some air and some sun, which he hasn't had for a long time. They have all sorts of stuff around the place, knitted furry pictures, soft toys and even a bus stop. As we were looking around, I saw a lady who said to one of the carers that she wanted to catch a bus. She looked slightly distressed, so he gave her 50p for her bus fare. She took the money and then a moment later completely forgot about it and wandered calmly off into one of the sitting rooms.

It's a big place with a few different seating areas, some with TVs and radios. There's a kitchen for the residents to use and also a big yellow dining room. There are regular activities going on such as music, singing and cooking. They have a policy of putting a picture frame on the bedroom doors, into which the family can put photos of their relative as they were in their former life. They also encourage the families to make 'memory books'. These are made up of photos which can be used to help the residents remember familiar people and places. Brian only remembers the distant past. He remembers his mum, who died when he was twenty, and the shop where they lived. Sometimes he doesn't know Margaret now, although he still sometimes says her name.

There was a bit of shouting from some of the residents which at first I found a bit shocking, and the place smells of wee, but on the whole the home looks like it would suit Brian because of the facilities it offers. And they want him out of the hospital now.

August 2009

3rd August

Brian moved to St Thomas' and is walking around and around again.

Skittles at the village hall. My arm is still really bad, so no skittling for me.

I had an appointment with a specialist at the Royal Berks Hospital who gave me a steroid injection in my shoulder to help with my 'Irritated Bursa'. In fact there were two very handsome specialists in the room, one using the ultrasound scanner and one with the needle. They located where to puncture me and the one with the injection stuck the needle in. He then decided he had got it in the wrong place and wiggled the needle to the right place. It was quite sore but I trustingly went off to become pain-free. They said it might hurt for a day or so but then should get better.

I have never been in so much pain in my entire life. For ten whole days I was in agony. The consultant rang to see how I was getting on and got a flea in his well-proportioned ear. Apparently steroid injections can work the opposite way.

September 2009

Brian is doing ok at St Thomas'. They boil-wash his clothes so they are now all brown. Margaret is not happy about this. She feels that it is very important for Brian to keep his dignity and look presentable, so she washes and irons all his clothes herself. Sometimes the residents take their slippers off where they sit and when they get up and wander off someone else will put them on. Items of clothing go missing too. Margaret has sewn labels into all his clothes but they still get put into other people's wardrobes. She is always having to mend tears to his pyjama button holes, which is telling of the struggle the carers must have getting him changed. They obviously don't have Margaret's negotiation skills.

He won't necessarily stay with us for very long when we visit; he walks off and we can't keep up with him because he walks so fast. Margaret takes a box of sweets with her to encourage him to stay with her a bit longer. The best thing is that she feels at ease talking to other families with loved ones at St Thomas' and says how good it is that they can all share the experience with each other. She is happy that Brian is being well cared for now.

I'm back working at George Palmer Primary School again with the little rascally Year 5 and 6s. Actually this time I have been given the 'gifted and talented' to work with and we are producing a cook book. The pupils' families and school staff have given us recipes to illustrate and, as it is a multi-cultural area, the recipes are quite unusual and interesting. The kids are using their IT skills to type up the recipes and are producing some very good artwork using collage, drawing and photography. We have a good budget which is always a beneficial factor when working in a 'deprived area', so we'll be able to produce an all-singing, all-dancing full-colour book.

I have started my numeracy level 2 course at Newbury College on a Tuesday evening. I didn't get a maths qualification at school; unfortunately I slipped through the net. Well, actually I tried very hard not to go to school on days when I had maths. I was a good actress and my mum usually fell for it. On the days when I did inadvertently go to school, I diligently queued up and asked my teachers for help, but they always said that they were too busy to help me. So in the end I gave up and just sat at the back and doodled on my exercise books for five years. My family were no help either. I even had the truant officer in to see me at one point, but all to no avail. They told my mum that I was 'highly strung'. That may have been so, but I thought all I needed was some help with my maths. And now I bloody well need a maths qualification on my job application forms, because otherwise it's embarrassing and a bit of a hindrance. Weirdly though, I'm now very much enjoying my numeracy classes. My teacher is as mad as a box of frogs but very clever, and has all the time in the world to help me.

21ˢᵗ December 2009. Snow.

I've got an interview with an education charity on Friday 8ᵗʰ January. They're called the 'Education Business Partnership West Berkshire' and run work-related events in primary and secondary schools. The role on offer is for a 'project officer covering maternity leave'. Funnily enough, the EBPWB office is just around the corner from Mr Clark's office at Greenham Common, so if I get the job we can travel to work together.

Went to the carol service at St Thomas' with Margaret. Sadly Brian doesn't want to sing any more. He did like the mince pies though.

Because of the snow, my interview date was postponed to Thursday 14th January.

January 2010

At my interview, I was shown into a very chilly room in a building that I found out later was used as the chapel and morgue for the Greenham Common airmen. I was interviewed for an hour and a half by two very friendly EBPWB ladies. We had a good chat and I answered all their questions. They asked me to write a mock press release as a test, which I duly did, but I was so cold my writing was really wobbly because I was shivering so much. I apologised and said that normally my handwriting wasn't as spidery. They understood and apologised for the room being so cold. I should have worn a vest.

Top tip* At job interviews wear layers as you never know what temperature you will be exposed to.

15th January

Michelle from the EBPWB rang to tell me that I had got the job. Apparently applicants had been thin on the ground. I start on 1st February.

February 2010

I've never had a proper job before and it isn't coming naturally to me. I can't believe I have to stay here in the office until 5pm – when then, and only then, I am allowed to go home. I feel like a caged animal. Luckily I sit opposite Aly who is my team leader. She laughs at me and is really kind; she also helps me out when I get in a fuddle with my Excel sheets. Chatty Lesley sits on the desk next to me. Lyn, who expertly deals with the NEETs (Not in Education, Employment or Training), sits over in the corner, and the ever-expanding Mel, whose seat I will take over shortly, is in the other corner. The trickiest task is to recruit business volunteers to help with the events that I will be project-managing and running in schools. I just have to find my way around the database, which nobody seems to be able to use anyway, and apparently I will have a lesson in shortly.

The boss says that I put the kettle on too often. I wondered how she knew as she hardly ever comes out of her office. She said that my shoes squeak. I bought some new shoes and now go round the other way to the kitchen. I can think better when I'm moving around but I don't think they'd understand. If only they had a ladder I could climb up and down, they'd get much more work out of me. The girls in the office don't mind regular cuppas though.

I'm not much good in meetings either – I get really fidgety as I don't like to sit down for too long and worry in case I say something stupid. Mr Clark has a similar thing, although the difference there is he really knows his stuff. Buzzword bingo isn't for him, he prefers plain-speaking. He says it makes him switch off and then his mind wanders, most likely to his next meal.

We found a bargain Cooke & Lewis kitchen at B&Q. 20% off all doors and drawers and then an extra 10% off the whole thing. It's very good-looking, a bit like a John Lewis of Hungerford kitchen but a whole lot cheaper. We chose nice handles and a few integrated baskets and are very pleased indeed, especially as we don't have to pay for it all at once.

Mr Clark has been made redundant from Telekinesis and on the one hand is very relieved, but on the other now has to find another contract. He has installed the kitchen and I am in raptures having kitchen cupboards and soft-close drawers. I am the one who travels to Greenham Common every day now and he makes the dinner in the evening. He's a pretty good cook and is making experimental dishes. He is also a big fan of

Masterchef, so I always say appreciatively, 'What a lovely plate of food,' in my best Greg Wallace voice. I think he's enjoying it. I know I am.

26th February

The Parish Plan youth film project screening at the village hall. Ta da.

With my job I regularly have to stand up in front of a whole room full of yawning year 10s to introduce the event we are running with them that day. I don't know why I bother – most of them aren't listening anyway. I'm really enjoying the job though, especially the days when we are in schools and not in the office sitting at a desk. We meet some very interesting people from all sorts of businesses who come along as volunteers to help the students.

I really like the people I work with, but the trouble with working in an office full of women is that they keep getting pregnant and showing you pictures of their ultrasound scans. I know they don't mean to upset me, but you'd think they'd spare a thought when they invite me to gather round their computer with my other cooing colleagues to view the full-screen picture. I don't want to seem rude, so I go and have a look and say something suitable. Then they have the audacity to bring the actual baby into the office when they've had it and pass it around, expecting you to have a hold.

It's all still a bit raw. It isn't their fault.

The *George Palmer Primary School Cook Book* has been formatted by my clever sis and we have had 100 copies printed. We held the grand unveiling at Waterstones in Reading with the participating children, the head teacher and the Mayor of Reading adorned in his golden chains. The manager at Waterstones said they will sell some copies for us in their local interest section. Good people.

We have a date for the VAT tribunal. Mr Clark has started making notes for our putting our case forward.

Appellants' arguments (us):

- The garage is separate to the main house and was used as a store as well as for car parking.

- Through the planning process we studied the rules on VAT closely. We didn't go as far as to study the VAT Act itself but we made sure we read all the documentation supplied to us by HMRC.

- We followed all the regulations and requirements but did not have any information given to us about what was and what was not allowable in regard to planning or tax matters. We had to trust that the information supplied to us was correct and factual. We proceeded in good faith that this was the case.

In fact nowhere did the information in our booklets mention garages.

April 2010

Our friend Phyllis died on 26th April and we went to her funeral. She was a huge part of the village and we will miss her. She was born in the village 83 years ago and must have seen a lot of changes through the years. Mr Clark was asked to operate the CD player at the church to play some Dusty Springfield tunes. She loved Dusty. Her flowers were made into the shape of a giant cigarette. At the graveside people threw cigarettes and lighters in with the coffin – I can imagine she would have been laughing her purple socks off. Around the same time, the Eyjafjallajökull volcano had erupted in Iceland and had caused chaos with its ash cloud. Her family made us all laugh by saying that it was probably Phyllis up there smoking a fag.

June 2010

15th June. A beautiful sunny day.

VAT Tribunal. London Tribunal Centre, Bedford Square.

Mr Clark and I took the day off work and travelled up to London. We got the train to Reading and then on to Paddington. Mr Clark won't go on the London Underground so we joined the taxi queue. I spotted Sir Ben Kingsley ahead of us in the queue and luckily Mr Clark didn't spot him. I remember when we went to Silverstone and Jackie Stewart walked past. Mr Clark said very loudly in a sort of Jeremy Clarkson voice 'JACKIE STEWART' … he is so embarrassing. Once we saw Danny Boyle at Heathrow and he did the same thing. I decided that on this occasion I would wait until we were safely installed in the taxi on our way to Bedford Square to tell him about it.

We arrived at a very smart-looking London townhouse and were asked to sign in at the door. We were shown into the waiting room. There were no frills – it was all very civil service – and as I sat there I imagined what it would have been like as a magnificent abode in the old days.

A short while later we were called into the court room where we shook hands with the Respondents, the Barrister Christiaan Zwart and his smart young solicitor with one earphone hanging out of his ear. They were very polite and we chatted as we waited for the judge.

Judge Roger Berner arrived with Miss Sheila Wong Chong FRICS and we all stood until they had processed past and had sat down, then we did the same. We had to represent ourselves as of course now we had no funds to have our own solicitor.

In the courtroom I stared at the old scenes of London which had slipped in their frames and then tried to look suitably intelligent by taking notes and nodding at appropriate moments in agreement with Mr Clark. I really hoped that I could keep it together and not embarrass Mr Clark in any way. I pressed my lips together in case I laughed or burped or did something else inappropriate. I don't know what it is about terrifyingly official occasions, it always makes me feel like I might lose control of myself and burst out somehow.

Mr Clark was very nervous but said that we believed that we had been misled by the HMRC. He said that we had read all the documents sent to us in the HMRC pack 'VAT refunds for DIY self-builders and converters Claim Pack', and that there was no reference anywhere to the exclusion of garages. He said as this was our first build, we relied on the information given to us and had not considered the necessity of looking at the VAT Act legislation itself. Even contacting the VAT helpline and talking to people at HMRC stands at shows did not bring to light any mention of the exception about garages.

They rejected the argument that we were misled by the HMRC on the grounds that we did not have enough specific evidence to question a claim based on 'legitimate expectation'. In other words they didn't give a stuff that we weren't given the information because they had never made a promise to anyone that they would provide it in the first place. (Very skilfully wriggled out of Judge Berner. One-nil to you.)

Mr Clark told them that the garage section, the part in question, was in fact less than 50% of the ground floor of the two-floor original building. The roof space was used only for storage, which meant that the total percentage of the building used for storage added up to 80%. This didn't seem to impress them.

Apparently, because we are self-builders, the 'Ultimate Consumer' and not in the building business, we are not readily entitled to zero-rated supplies. To make it less unfair though, section 35 VATA makes provision for self-builders to claim for a VAT refund on materials. Only under certain conditions however.

These conditions brought up questions and I was getting a numb bum and a bit fidgety.

Issue 1. Construction of the dwelling

Was Mr Clark's construction designed within section 35 (1A)(a) (new build)? Mr Clark said yes, and that was due to the collapse of a wall on the south-west elevation, which meant that there was only a single façade left standing (thanks to Nick and Ben the demolition demons). He then said that as it was a condition of the planning permission to keep the wall, it therefore ceased to be an existing building.

Were the works a residential conversion within section 35(1A) (c)? Mr Zwart said that clearly there was an existing building, so you couldn't say that the original building had ceased to exist.

But in our eyes, the fact remained that even though the existing building was not completely demolished to ground level, by virtue of the planning permission condition to keep one façade, and even though it wasn't an explicit condition, the original building did then in fact cease to exist.

Mr Zwart was very kind in not pursuing this further.

Was the wall that collapsed during building then built up again with the same bricks? Mr Clark said that even though it was rebuilt it cannot be described as part of the original building. The HMRC concurred.

I had to keep pressing my stomach in with my hand as it was rumbling very loudly. Normally I would have had elevenses by now.

Issue 2. Residential conversion or not?

They then said that if the build does not qualify as a new build, Mr Clark could still qualify for a refund if the building was a conversion of a non-residential building or a non-residential part of a building.

As they now knew that the original building was 80% non-residential we were hopeful.

Other previous cases were discussed and the merits in relation to our case were considered.

The court broke for lunch and we all stood and let the judge and Miss Wong Chong out first. Mr Clark and I bought a sandwich and a drink from the deli round the corner and sat in the sun on a bench with the pigeons in Bedford Square.

After lunch we all filed back in, standing again for the entrance of Judge Berner and Miss Wong Chong.

In conclusion they said they will allow the appeal, 'subject to an adjustment to exclude from Mr Clark's claim VAT attributable to the conversion of the garage area'. So we will see what they come up with.

We were very grateful to Mr Zwart for not wiping the floor with us. He could have very easily.

After it was over, we all shook hands again and went our separate ways. Mr Clark and I tootled off to the British Museum to decompress. We had a look at the Rosetta Stone, which is probably easier to decipher than the VAT Act.

We had to walk for miles to get a taxi back to Paddington, all the way to the Tottenham Court Road in fact. I grumbled all the way. My smart shoes were rubbing and the balls of my feet were on fire. I'm not used to wearing heels now. Mr Clark declined to give me a piggyback, which I thought was a bit much.

In the summary of our case they wrote:

> Mr Clark appeared in person. HMRC were represented
> by Christiaan Zwart. We are grateful to them both for

their helpful submissions; to Mr Zwart for his helpful summary of the background and underlying law and to Mr Clark who, despite the daunting task of dealing with the legislation that, whilst designed to assist the layman, is less than user friendly, nevertheless presented his case clearly and with some skill.

I am so proud.

HMRC wrote to us and offered us 50% so we wrote back and said that we didn't agree with their decision, so we'll have to go back to the court again. I will wear sensible shoes.

July 2010

28th July

I took the morning off from a careers fair at a school to do my maths level 2 exam. I was very nervous but completed all the questions, much to my relief. I'll just have to wait and see if I got any of them right.

August 2010

6th August

Our fifth wedding anniversary.

Surprisingly, Mr Clark and I went to see the musical *Copacabana* at the Watermill Theatre in Newbury. I say surprisingly because Mr Clark isn't known for his love of musicals; I think he just went along because I wanted to go and for the promise of dinner beforehand. His mum recently bought him a DVD of *Seven Brides for Seven Brothers* as she thought it might change his mind. He tried to watch it but turned it off after a minute or so as it really didn't do anything for him. You should see his face pucker at the merest suggestion of *The Wizard of Oz*. *Copacabana*, however, turned out to be a revelation for him. The Watermill is a really small and cosy theatre, and all the actors played instruments, danced, acted and sang. He was really very impressed. It was capped off for both of us with a spooky coincidence in the story which started out with a couple who were celebrating their fifth wedding anniversary. Oo-er. The cast were a bit taken aback by the enthusiasm of the audience after the finale – they wouldn't let them go until they had sung *Copacabana* one more time … we've both been singing it ever since.

I passed my maths level 2 exam. What joy.

September 2010

Am pregnant again.

23rd September

We went back to the court in Bedford Square, all previous attendants attending. Mr Clark hadn't had that much time to prepare this time but reiterated that he felt that we were entitled to around 81% of our claimed sum. He said this was because the garage area in question was only about 19% (18.6% to be exact) of our completed building. In the original building, the garage area was 28.05 metres and now, with the extension of the building, the overall floor area is 150.4 metres. In financial terms this would mean £1,716.92 of our original claim of £9,230.74. Mr Clark said that they therefore owed us £7,514.82.

Mr Zwart said that in regard to section 35 and note (8) of Group 5 of Schedule 8 VATA, the apportionment should be related to the original building and not the completed building. He said it should also be calculated by volume and not just by floor space. We could see his point, but ...

The finding was that the refund should be determined by what is deemed to be the residential and non-residential parts of the building, including the roof space.

The roof space over the garage, according to the 'application of the facts', is deemed to be part of the garage so they will only give us 50% of our claimed sum.

October 2010

Am not pregnant anymore.

Game over.

⬭ ⊘ ⊗

November 2010

10th November

We received a letter from HMRC to say that a bank giro for £4,747.37 will follow from the National Payment Centre.

⬭ ⊘ ⊗

At this point Kevin would now ask us how much the build actually cost. We would be a bit evasive and give him a round-about estimate, probably 10 or 20% under what we actually spent to save embarrassment.

Now I can get that Mazda MX5 I have had my eye on.

EPILOGUE

June 2014

Margaret and Brian have moved away to Hertford to be near her family. She is living in a house which is part of a complex specially built for older folk. Brian has his own room in the nursing home next door. Margaret can see his window from her front door and she can visit him anytime she likes now. Tanzy the little Jack Russell is looking quite old but has adapted to her new surroundings quite well, although she now only has 8 or so square metres on which to do her 'puddles' and number twos. I expect she's wondering where the big garden has gone where she used to chase aeroplanes and bark at hedgehogs.

Brian is stuck in a body that has forgotten how to move and his eyes have forgotten how to focus. He just looks up. I've witnessed his frustration when he shouts, trying to communicate a fleeting glimpse of something, who knows what, that has just shot through his synapses and off again into the ether. His eyes water with emotion, perhaps rage.

He still eats well. He's like a baby, the spoon goes to his lips and he opens his mouth. His room is light and airy and there is no smell of wee anywhere in the building. The whole place feels calm.

We gave Margaret a CD Walkman and she plays Brian his favourite hymns. She says that as he listens, she can see his eyes change and his whole being become peaceful. She strokes his cheeks and combs his hair which he obviously enjoys.

Alzheimer's is the worst of all robbers. It has taken Brian bit by bit until there is hardly anything left of him. His engine has been stolen and only the rolling stock remains. I only hope someone has left the radio on in one of the carriages.

The house needs redecorating inside and out. Some things never got finished. Some of the settling cracks got fixed but some are still unpainted. The carpets need cleaning. The weather has forced its way through the oak screen, making tannin stains; the lock on the downstairs loo is still broken, and we never did get used to the light switch being on the wrong side of the door. It still makes us swear, every time.

The Olivieri boiler is excellent but we still have reservations about leaving it on when we go out. Our neighbours over the road have got used to it now; at first they thought our house was on fire as it makes such a glow with its flickering flame. All the problems we had with it not lighting or running properly turned out to be a motor that needed a bit of lubrication – a simple fix diagnosed and executed by Mr Clark's genius friend Frank Decmar.

Mr Clark turned 50 this month and still has no grey hair, but does have some rogue eyebrow hairs which I pluck out with my tweezers. His old band 'The Deckchairs' all turned 50 too and they played a reunion gig at the Purple Turtle bar in Reading. They enjoyed it so much they have decided to carry on with their rehearsals, so I told Mr Clark in no uncertain terms to go and buy some earplugs. His hearing is quite bad already and I don't want to have to shout at him to go and get a hearing aid and then sit there listening to it whistling. They are playing at the 'Rebellion Punk Festival' this year up in Blackpool which he is very excited about.

I had to leave the EBPWB due to funding cuts and have since been doing the odd portrait commission, teaching art evening classes and working at a local primary school. My Year 3s are giving me hell but I am learning to take no prisoners.

Mr Clark has just finished a contract for Jaguar Land Rover and I have unpinned the house 'still to do' list from the cork board, where it has languished silently for the past six years. I haven't been able to do much more work on the house myself as my neck and shoulder are still quite bad. Mr Clark and Mr Williams' electric bike business is still chugging along, yet to make its big break, but they won't give in.

Mr Clark is still on the parish council and the village hall committee and I am now booking clerk for the village hall. We'll be getting a new hall soon, as the current one, even though it has a certain charm, is a rat-infested and mouldy WW1 Canadian army hut in danger of being condemned. In common with most villages we have some bubbling undercurrents of unrest and resistance to change, and a particularly annoying vexatious complainer; but we still have our good friends, although some have now moved away or sadly passed away.

The Pickle is doing really well and has turned into a beautiful, well-balanced and brainy 14-, very nearly 15-year-old. She is one of the loveliest people I know. She goes to a great school where the girls all have regulation-height ponytails. She says they start school in the first year with their hair all over the place, but soon fall into line. It is a shame that I only get to see her in the school holidays when she comes over. She still doesn't stay over. Mr Clark picks her up after school every Tuesday and they go to Waitrose for a coffee. Sometimes I give him a shopping list so that they can wander round the shop together; that way he gets to spend more time with her and she gets more chocolate.

We lost another baby in 2012, but who was I kidding? I was 47 for heaven's sake. The door has been securely bolted so they can't get in now. I will turn 50 next year and thankfully the desire to have a child has completely gone.

The house has hold of my soul. Mr Clark and I feel the same way. We find it difficult to leave when we go away and a great sense relief to come home again. When we return, I rush in and shout, 'It's ok everybody, we're home!' like the house might have missed us and is breathing a sigh of relief. A fanciful thought I know but our collective thoughts and decisions have made our home what it is and we belong in every fibre.

Visitors say that the house has a relaxed atmosphere and smells really nice. I think it's because they come in through the lobby straight into the kitchen and dining room with all its foody smells and oak woodwork and windows. The vista is a verdant walled garden, now with its fig tree just coming into leaf, a great big peony bush just about to burst forth, marigolds and courgette plants in the vegetable bed, and wheat grass and weeds in the gravel around the bird table.

We feel very lucky indeed to be here. God bless you Margaret and Brian.

†

1ˢᵗ September 2014

Margaret died suddenly at the weekend. Mr Clark and I are heartbroken. She had just got her new home in order and was looking forward to an easier life, with more time for herself.

She didn't get the chance to read my finished book, but did recently come back to the village and sat with me at my computer to read through what I had written about her and Brian. She helped me to get the facts completely right, and was very happy that their story might be of use to people whose relatives have Alzheimer's, and that it would also increase awareness and understanding of the disease.

We are still in shock and will miss her incredibly. We have so many fond memories of our friendship, which we will treasure forever.

Acknowledgements

Thank you John Clark for your patience and help with writing the book, even though I know you would have rather been playing your guitar or watching *Mighty Ships*.

Thank you Mummy Monkcom for letting me riffle through your diaries, for lending me your ear and for laughing in all the right places.

Thank you Deborah Bosley for your inspiration and encouragement, your editing skills and for sharing your cakes with me.

Thank you Kate Northover for your fabulous book cover design, your kind help with proofreading and editing, and for being my best sis.

Thank you Papa Monkcom for your creative ideas, your humour and encouragement and also for your delicious dinners.

Thank you Sue Monkcom for giving me your support, advice, and kind words of encouragement.

Thank you Kerry Hughes for proofreading the book, and for giving me a boost with your enthusiasm for my project.

Thank you Richard Ingrams for not laughing at me when I said that I was writing a book, and for pointing me in the right direction.

Thank you Pea Brodhurst for passing on your valuable knowledge about self-publishing a book.

Thank you Catherine Dodds for being so generously supportive in steering me through the publishing process, and for formatting the book.

Thank you Jenni Collins for your marketing advice, your cheeriness and your help with getting my social media up and running.

Thank you Margaret Davey, wherever you are, for making it all possible and changing our lives.

Mandy Clark
by Mandy Monkcom